unalone

ALSO BY THE AUHOR

Take Me with You, Wherever You're Going

Pelvis with Distance

CO-AUTHOR

Write It! 100 Poetry Prompts to Inspire

unalone

POEMS IN CONVERSATION
WITH THE BOOK OF GENESIS

JESSICA JACOBS

FOUR WAY BOOKS
TRIBECA

LIBRARY OF CONGRESS CATALOGING-IN-PUBLICATION DATA

Names: Jacobs, Jessica, 1980- author.
Title: Unalone : poems in conversation with the Book of Genesis / Jessica
  Jacobs.
Description: New York, New York : Four Way Books, 2024.
Identifiers: LCCN 2023031736 (print) | LCCN 2023031737 (ebook) | ISBN
  9781954245822 (trade paperback) | ISBN 9781954245839 (ebook)
Subjects: LCGFT: Poetry.
Classification: LCC PS3610.A356433 U53 2024 (print) | LCC PS3610.A356433
  (ebook) | DDC 811/.6--dc23/eng/20230714
LC record available at https://lccn.loc.gov/2023031736
LC ebook record available at https://lccn.loc.gov/2023031737

This book is manufactured in the United States of America and printed on acid-free paper.

Four Way Books is a not-for-profit literary press. We are grateful for the assistance
we receive from individual donors, public arts agencies, and private foundations
including the NEA, NEA Cares, Literary Arts Emergency Fund, and the
New York State Council on the Arts, a state agency.

We are a proud member of the Community of Literary Magazines and Presses.

CONTENTS

These sections follow the twelve פָּרְשִׁיּוֹת *parshiyot (portions) of Genesis, which are each named for the portion's first distinctive word or phrase. The notes provide brief summaries of the biblical stories and other relevant sources.*

וַיֵּצֵא ◦ *VAYETZEI* ◦ (AND HE LEFT)

וַיִּשְׁלַח ◦ *VAYISHLACH* ◦ (AND HE SENT)

וַיֵּשֶׁב ◦ *VAYESHEV* ◦ (AND HE SETTLED)

מִקֵּץ ◦ *MIKETZ* ◦ (AT THE END OF)

וַיִּגַּשׁ ◦ *VAYIGASH* ◦ (AND HE DREW NEAR)

וַיְחִי ◦ *VAYECHI* ◦ (AND HE LIVED)

Notes

To Burt Visotzky

רב וחבר

rav v'haver
(teacher and friend)

Like the One who has no mouth, who spoke the first letter that has no sound, the biblical word conceals an infinity of meanings.

—Lawrence Kushner

To read, to listen, to write, to feel, to fear, to draw courage from others, to take risks, to wrestle with contradictions, to engage with others—this is, indeed, the verb without tenses, the conversation without an end.

—Adrienne Rich

Stepping through the Gate

Make a fence, said the rabbis, *around the Torah.* And this world
is lousy with them. More than we can count
on our dogwalk alone: chainlink and iron and white
wooden pickets. Fences to keep people's bad barking dogs

in, to keep our bad barking dog out. His nostrils flare
wide as a twirled skirt as he reads the tales of past passersby
on fences that mark what is another's burden, another's
privilege to tend, and what is open to the traffic of strangers.

Called up to the Torah, a reader tracks the cramped letters
with a יד *yad*—a metal pointer topped by a tiny pointing hand.
If it feels colder than the air, it's because silver steals
your body's heat, this tool to keep your place, keep you

in your place, to keep you from marring even a single sacred letter.
This, one fence among many: Do not bring the Torah
in the bathroom, do not sit beside it on a bench, do not stand before it
naked (lest you be buried naked, stripped of all the good you did).

But sometimes barriers grow so large it's hard to see
what they're protecting. And here is the fig tree yearning
past its yard, reaching toward the walk with its fat-fingered leaves.
Here, the arbor propping branches hunched as the shoulders

of a weary giant—yet under its slump, an exuberance
of mulberries. There, the yellow house whose bramble is more
than worth its thorns: like drops of ink dripping from the branches,
the blackberries call us to make a quill of our tongues.

Let every fence in my mind have a gate.
With an easy latch and well-oiled hinges. The neighbors

urge us to indulge—*There's more than we can possibly eat*—
so, here, love, is fruit with the sun still inside it. Let me

thumb the juice from your chin. Let us honor what we love
                                        by taking it in.

בְּרֵאשִׁית

≅

Bereshit

≅

(In the Beginnings)

In the beginnings

light needs creating—darkness
is already here. Commingled,
this first light looks
like a sandstorm
    maybe: everything
        at once: quavering and resonant
           as a plucked string
              until God commences the ceremony
              of separations—light
            from dark, terebinths
             from touch-me-nots, Florida
              from the Gulf and sea, אָדָם *adam*

              from אֲדָמָה *adamah* (earth), Adam
            from חַוָּה *Chava* (mother
          of us all), asps
         and whistlepigs
        and hellbenders
      from them both. God,
    who in this beginning
is אֱלֹהִים *Elohim* (God of Judgment), knows
when there is nothing but light, nothing
can be seen. So now there's nothing
unmet by shadow. Knows
that to say *I am*
    is to be strengthened

but also severed
from all
        not you.

Mystics say everything God
makes is made of God. Creation

in and of its Creator, just as each of us
remains our mother's child: once helpless,
sheltered, and cradled through the air. But as Brazil was once

spooned by Cameroon before the continents began their drift—
who can remember that union? With all things
separate and their selves, what wonders!
                    Yet we are left
                 with such need
              of connection, bereft
in all our lonesome splendor.

"And God said, 'Let there be light!' and there was light."

—Genesis 1:3

And God speaks

words that enter the world
as things. Says, אוֹר *Ohr!* (light)

before מָאוֹר *Ma'ohr!* (source of light)
because the word
is its own illumination.

Says, *Fig tree!* and the soil
ripples with sudden roots
while the wind finds leaves

to riffle. Says, *Cattle!* and there
is the hot green breath
of rumination, says, *Birds!* and

a white egret paces the bull's back,
plucking ticks from his hide. Each word
carries what it names inside

and, like a folded paper flower
blooming in water, finds its form
in the moment of its speaking.

*"And God created the large sea creatures, and every living creature
that moves, with which the waters swarmed, after their kind . . . And
God saw that it was good."*

—Genesis 1:21

Prayer should be a tunnel

my Hebrew teacher says, and I find myself pigtailed, a kid again,
descending from a blazing Florida day into the murky depths
of SeaWorld's Tunnel of Terror: a massive glass

passage through a seawater tank. Sharks glide by,
fins foxed and furrowed as the edges of old treasure maps.
Far above, the inaccessible surface

ripples a chainmail of light. *Prayer should be
a tunnel*, she says again, making an *O*
of her hands and pushing it out before her—my teacher,

also a dancer, uses her body to create structures
in the air. *It should take you there*, she says. English
is not her first language, but by *there*, I know

she means *God*. By *tunnel*, I think she means
conduit, a direct channel in. Divine umbilical. A sign
in line showed a whale teetering atop

one of the tunnel's glass blocks to demonstrate
its fortitude, to tell me not to be afraid. But I am,
each shark with its hacksaw teeth clearly meant

for me, and it's only a matter of time before one
gnaws its way through, bringing all the water
rushing in. And what would happen first—

drowning or being devoured? For those, like me, rooted
in terror, a moving sidewalk keeps us in motion,
easing us through the eerie underpass, acting just like

time, which moves us without the need for us
to move, which moves us whether or not we want it to.
Prayer should be a tunnel, she says, but what words,

what melody, would let me make with my body
such grand architecture in the air, let me stand
in one place and travel both out and in, let me sink

and not drown, let me wander unafraid
into the open mouth and emerge
                              unscathed and changed?

Creation Stories

In the original, Adam has my back—
is my back—our bodies
one body. We take turns
walking forward. As each
sees half the world, we
see it all: minds a communal
well, our only blind spot
is the other's face. When he is tired,
I sleep; when I am hungry,
he eats. But our hunger
                              ends there.
For him, for me, there is no need
for longing. You do not crave
your own elbow.

In the remake, we're
separate. His eyes the color
of damp earth. To know his mind,
I must now ask questions; he gives me
a name so he can call for me. Language
is our first child. Rib of his cage,
face to my face, we are creative
in the ways we rebind ourselves. Again,
when I am hungry, he eats. Old habits
die hard. But he does know the rules. So
when I offer the fruit and he accepts

it means he marries me: makes
my death his death; my future, ours.
Eden could have been his alone;
I am the paradise he chose.

"Thorns and thistles will sprout for you when you seek to eat the grasses
of the field; by the sweat of your brow shall you get bread to eat."
—*Genesis 3:18-19*

Imposter Syndrome Among the Thorns and Thistles

How old were you, when the world tipped
its hand? When things you thought were natural
showed their seams? I was thirteen. On trucked-in pallets
across the street, squares of scutch grass
stacked high as my head. Did you know a lawn
could be delivered? I didn't, but lured by promises
of doing with the same work as the boys,
I hauled and placed, puzzling them neat
as a sheet of graph paper.

                  The girls that year had begun
to paint their faces, a line of cheap orange stark
along their jaws. Unlike me, they had not yet learned the art
of how to blend: all those boys I pretended to like, all the girls
I pretended not to. In thrift stores, we tried on others'
past-season selves—the clothes, like the kids in the hallways,
grouped by color and type. We wore masks of slang and song lyrics,
dropped band names like currency, smoked skunk weed
copped from an older brother's underwear drawer. Mirrors held
a special magnetism: Instead of homework, I studied myself.
Remembered synagogue as something forced
to attend; prayers as soundtracks for the lives of other people.

And after school, I walked home past the grass, the contrived
squares busy stitching and joining into a lawn, passing
themselves off like they'd been there all along. Yet I could still
feel the weight of that sod, the wet itch of it on my skin, the wonder
that wherever I set it, that patch would bind itself
to the ground below.

                    All day, my neighbors' sprinklers stuttered covenants
of rainbows. All night, to the hiss of their groundwater whispers,
I traced out my new hips and breasts, the possibilities
I might grow into.

And now, decades on, I'm trying to grow a lawn
on me, to zip myself into Judaism
like a patchwork parka of grass, hoping it might take
hold, might one day fit snug as a golf course greenway.

                    Outside, the lawn; inside, me: Were both fake
because I'd helped make them?
                                        If something is worked for
                                        can it still be true?

Sleepwalkers in the Garden

At least afterward, Adam and Eve knew
what they'd lost. Knew their bodies
as separate, which gave them something

to long for. Knew God—that companion
who'd strolled beside them in the appled
evenings—as a whispering in the quiet
corner of their chests: a new reason
to be still and listen.

                    When my grandmother
moaned into the pain of her final days, there
were her bottom teeth—those pickets, the same
irregular thicket as mine. Her eyes, the same
too, only flecked with the green of new leaves.

Why had it taken until then to see? Paradise
is every moment we've ever left, all the small
unnoticed gardens we can never again enter.

"God said to Cain . . . 'Where you do right, there is uplift, but where you do not, sin crouches at your door; it longs for you, but you can rule over it.'"

—Genesis 4:6-7

Free will

is in our hands: in these bones lashed
by ligaments, sheathed

in skin. Flex your fingers wide; like folding fans,
collapse them in. Muscleless puppets,

they are merciless or tender depending
on what moves them. We can train

a single finger to hold a body's weight; all ten
together, to summon a sonata, birth a baby, ball

into clubs and beat a man to death. We tatters
of lace and crafters of skyscrapers

are the only animals who can make a fist.
How much simpler if our bodies' weapons

were separate, obvious as antlers. Yet,
the Talmud speaks of יֵצֶר הָרַע *yetzer ha'ra,*

our "evil inclination," as the source
of all creativity and desire—the same urge a spur

to make love or take someone
without consent, toward righteous anger

or violent rage. Like the rabbis, some states
define a deadly weapon only

after the fact, by the damage
a thing caused. Like *break* is both

opportunity and *fracture*, as *cleave*
holds fast while it also splits apart,

our hands—these striving hymns
of contranyms.

At Age 969, Methuselah Gives a Valedictory Address

In the beginning, each day was bright
as a new coin and fit for spending. Now?
Nothing is allowed to be exquisitely itself.

Even a kiss is a trotline heavy with hooks,
trawling up all kisses past.
Perhaps God isn't omniscient, just old

enough all patterns are laid bare. Our lives
not preordained, only predictable:
how even empty rooms are now crowded

with my dead. Yet when I was
a pair of grass-greened knees, even the birds
seemed to ask, *What do you want to be*

when you grow up? As though transformation
were possible. But my metamorphosis
was the ordinary kind: that boy

into this man. Still, I hope
some mystery remains. May the grass
that soon grows from me whisper

all the answers I wish I'd given: *A warm temple*
in a wintry place. A welcoming bed for those I love best.
A lake deep enough to hold all our longing.

"[And God said to Cain,] 'Cursed are you from the ground that opened its mouth to take your brother's blood from your hand.'"
—Genesis 4:10-11

And the Ground Opens Its Mouth to Speak

Dear wandering dust, dear vagrant clay,
dear humans made of me,

how quickly you've forgotten.
I am not just a backdrop
for your horrors—

read your holy book: Stars and trees
join in battle, hills mourn, valleys
and waves shudder and writhe

at the approach of God. And how
many of your slaughtered
have I choked down?

Your clearcuts evict owls,
salamanders, wolves so you can build
your houses in hills now primed

for fire. I am trying
to warn you. For every season,
I send wrong weather, drain

reefs of their color, let whole species
go extinct. Yet you go on.
Enough. Too much.

Protagonist, delinquent. Who are you
in this story:

Seeing something he wanted
across the road, a boy dropped
his mother's hand

and ran into the snarl
of traffic. She screamed his name,
rooted there, unable to look away.

At the clamor and rush, at a mirror hissing
so close past his ear it raised
the small hairs inside it,

he ran back to her. Weeping,
she slapped him, hard; weeping,
he pressed the heat of his cheek

to her chest. That slap? Pain now
to stave off worse later. A mark
to carry with him and remember.

I am so tired of being afraid
for you.

Before the Beginning

Once there was one:

a pilot flame—tiny blue spark of every being
who'd ever flycreepswimrunbloom
                                    flickering in that dark light.

    Creation demanded distinctions. Chaos and void
tamed into sea and shore and sky; night
exiled from day.

                       No longer
             one and wedded,
there were distances in need
            of crossing.
                Which made time,
                conflict, language,
                and desire.
So the world is
because we can know it as nothing
else. We place a glass on a table
            and need it
not to fall through.

              Yet even faces are just a guise
of cells compliant to their fates. Hair,
skin, tooth, bone—look closer
still: a loose union of matter
            sprinting through space.

    Yes,
your walls, yes, my walls, yet something inside us remembers
                  and trembles.

נֹחַ

≅

Noach

≅

(Noah/Rest)

The Hebrew תֵּבָה *tayva, normally translated as* "ark,"
can also mean "word."

Collective Nouns

א.

When Noah was still
    just a man, not yet sailor and savior,
God said,

> *Make yourself a word,*
> *for I have decided to silence*
> *all flesh.*

  Scraping muscle
    from a hide, his wife
  crouched nearby, listening.

Without argument or question, without a single
signal of warning to neighbors or friends,
her husband—that little wind-up toy, God's docile
errand boy—complied. He built the word
to spec: big enough to hold
two of every creature,
but too small for her
    mother, too small for her brother, no matter
        how she wept.

ב.

From planks of gopher wood smeared with pitch,
Noah built the word and God shut them up
in it.

Water crushed down from the sky, fountained from the seas, dissolving
living dust and breath
        to reefs of hushed mud.

                  And Noah:
           a silent man in a silenced world,
            drifting in a wooden word.

ג.

With an otter placid as a stole across his shoulders,
instead of talking,
     he lived in his hands, picking
   nits; troughing food and water, always more water; tending,
tending to every walking, creeping, winged thing, to all beings
but her—never lying beside her, never tasting
the taste of sleep, his tongue
withered to a husk.

The dark hold was mobbed with chitter, roar, and screech
         without restraint, and from outside, the ceaseless babble
of wood and rain. She was drowning
in languages she couldn't speak, and he never offered her
a word
     of comfort.

ז.

When the rains finally ended, Noah bound a rope to the rafters.
Before the raven, before the doves, he lowered himself
from the word's one window. A splash,
and he leashed the rope to his ankle; leaned
back and let his hands fall empty, let the flood
               embrace him.

Grime sloughed from him into the waves
until the only animal he smelled
　　　was himself. Noah
　　　　　　　　bobbed there, a beaming buoy,
　　　　　　tethered to the word
　　　　　in which the future
floated, where his wife, unseen—the new Eve, humanity's
unnamed mother—looked out from the window and watched
　　　as he gave himself to the killing waters;
　　　　　looked past him, trying not to think
　　　　　　　　of the death and rot that brothed him.

ה.

Is a man good,
　　　　　she wondered,
　　　　who can construct a word
　　　　　　　　　large enough
　　　　　for only
　　　　　　　　a chosen few?

ו.

And now, no matter what promise
once rainbowed the sky, before the world
is again silenced—the water and weather
　　　　　already rising, already tearing the roofs
　　　　from the poorest among us—
　　　instead of floating
　unnoticing past those taken by the tides,
　　　　　can't we build a peaceful fleet,
　　　lashed by syntax and spring lines
into a sentence of survival:
　　　　　　words that welcome
　　　　　not just some, but
　　　　　　　　all?

As the waters of the Flood receded and the earth began to dry, God
called forth Noah and his family from the ark, along with all the living
creatures within.

And God speaks

a covenant
like a sudden island

in a formless sea,
like a tent

on that steady shore,
which, lit

by the light
you kindle

within, is a glowing
lung in the night

bellowed
by your breathing

what was once
God's breath—

easy to forget
until it's time

to return it.

After the Flood

Across the evergreen field
of the felt-topped basement table,
God, alone, deals another hand.

How quiet the house is
empty. And Solitaire less play than lonely
puzzle, a time-passing contest of dealer
versus deck: no matter how you wish
the cards, you take them as they are,
which is why this game's other name
is Patience.
            One turn begets
              another, each of us arranged
by suit and rank—however we might fight
our fates, or rail against that bad-faith covenant:
no more floods, but, *sure, why not?* to pandemics
and mass extinctions. Because lord knows
there are so many ways to go under.

When what we've created is far
from how we've planned—
little images of God, we
understand that surge and relief
at disappointment's release,
the Great Arm's
volatile flash, dashing it all,
                    yet again, from the table.

Just past the ground-level windows,
sprinklers hiss counterfeit rainbows.
Inside, paint veils
      the brown bullseye of ceiling-seep,

the wall-drawn lines of receded floodwaters,
but can't touch the funk of mildew.
                                        Some hurts
cannot be hidden. And trust, after betrayal, is not belief
but hope—a feeling without foundation.

Across the evergreen field,
God, alone, deals another hand.

Elegy in Prophetic Perfect

Like God saying, *You have entered the ark,*
before Noah cut a single plank,

or saying, at Sinai, *I make this covenant*
with those here

and those not here, as in *with those*
to come—a promise

transcending the present. It's the tense
of done and dusted, of bet

your ass and bottom dollar, of here
now though not quite yet.

Like Joseph saying to a prosperous
Pharaoh, *And there were seven years*

of famine, as though he'd already
seen that devastation, already

heard the pleading in the streets. A vision
of the future so certain

it's already past. Like my mother,
decades before

she would forget her own name
or the fact she'd had children, saying,

You'll miss me when I'm gone.

In the Shadow of Babel

To run along the Hudson is to pass through ghosts
of the Meal Market, where grains were sold
beside Native and African captives. Then inland,
between the skyscrapers of Wall Street, where
even in high summer, alleys are shaded to night and cold
as snowmelt streams. Which makes it easy to believe
men-who-would-be-gods once built a tower
to rival the heavens, laid the foundation
while seaweed creped the remnants of redwoods
and dolphins rotted in mountain lakes—
the Flood not myth but memory,
their desire to build beyond drowning
sensible. Yet as one generation built
on the next, citizens were muscled
into one mold, indivisible, indistinguishable
as the clay bricks they passed from hand to hand
in that assembly line to the sky. *And the whole earth
was of one language*: However differently they felt it,
people had to speak their pain the same.

∞

But what does such pain mean to me
who runs with no one chasing her, with no one lying
in wait—to a woman running
simply because she wants to?

The past is a tower tall enough to pierce
                time, transmit
all echoes, to continue
                    casting shadows.

∞

To the west, Manifest Destiny of corn-soy-cotton-wheat
displaces all that once grew there with uniform
grids of green and the need for labor to tend them—
the old whisk-away-the-tablecloth trick
done cruelly, so few people left standing.

      Africans branded with their captors' initials,
   then again, with the surnames
of their buyers.

        Native children dragged
from Sha'note, "wind blowing through,"
to Charlotte; Lone Bear
to Lon Brown.

      Names that meant
nothing, in letters they couldn't read.

To the east, *Blut und Boden, Blood and Soil*: a swastika
crossed by a sword and sheaf of wheat.

      Jews issued IDs stamped with a red *J*
   and new middle names:
Israel for men, *Sarah* for women. Then,
in the camps, shorn to nothing
but numbers.

Fleeing pogroms, vowing to send
for his wife and young son,
at Ellis Island, alone,

      my great-grandfather immigrated
from Kudlanski to Goodman.

∞

Like plants smothered by a tarp to cleanse the land
   for the one crop deemed desirable.
Like my grandparents' Polish, Yiddish, and Hebrew,

like the ancestors no one speaks of
massacred in a Polish synagogue, or in a pit in a forest
they were forced to dig themselves—many of them
farmers who knew what it was to dig, who knew
the good such work could bring.
Like their murders I know only from the archives.

Monoglot me, struggling to speak, to listen
to what, to who came before:

      Generic American, protected
    by my passing

as not Jewish, not queer;
so often oblivious.

      Though Charlemagne said, *To have another language,*
      is to possess a second soul,

to have the language of your home
is to possess the soul that is your own.

∞

As those enslaved were forced to speak
the colonists' language—even that corner
of their minds colonized.
      As *Kill the Indian, Save*
      the Man meant severing
children from their homes, severing
their braids, forcing them into shoes and faith and words
that wouldn't fit.
      As Nazis burned sacred texts,
        trying to bonfire the holy
tongue from Jews' mouths.

As they were torn
from their parents
on auction blocks and reservations,
at borders and in selection lines—children,
those words we say to the future.

∞

With no child, with only English,
I feel severed from every time
but the present and question
what brings me, now, to speak:

Because a president praised
rabid men who chanted, *Blood and soil*,
chanted, *Jews will not replace us*, chanted
with their pink faces flushed and raging
in the flicker of tiki torches?
Because I finally know
the feeling that the country I was born in is mine
but not meant for me?

It took this fear to grow
my voice.

∞

Two-thirds of the world
now speaks English, every culture
bound. Without firebreaks,
a single strain of hatred
can inflame the world.

Here, murders in synagogues,
in the homes of rabbis; beatings

in the streets. On the way to shul, Jews hide
yarmulkes under baseball caps, pry
mezuzahs from their doors.

                  Out for a jog, on a walk to the store, in the car
with their kids, in their own backyards and beds,
Black men and women, Black children, murdered
by those paid to protect them,
                    by those who forced
Water Protectors into dog kennels at Standing Rock
after scrawling arrest numbers on their arms.

∞

America—always
    a grander city, always a more
                    towering tower
           built on land
    stolen from those who listened to it
            well enough to know
when dogwood leaves are the size of a squirrel's ear,
sow corn. When lilacs bloom, seed the beans
whose roots will feed the cornstalks that support them.
And once those purples fade, plant squash: a sprawl
of broad green ground cover. Each plant providing
what the other requires.

                 At Babel, God said,
"Let us נָבְלָה *navlah* their language"—"to confound"
but also "to intermingle."

Let the world tell us
what the world needs and when.

∞

While the nights are still cold
in my new mountain home,
 I join our neighbors to ready the ground
with pickaxe and spade, to jostle
rocks from their strangle of roots
and turn the dirt with the rich heat of humus
grown from the scraps of our tables and yards;
we water the starts and tuck them gently
in the soil.

And during the summer harvest,
                    in this garden open
              to all who want to work there,
       the light so late shadows
grow weary of waiting and slink off
to sleep in corners—with hands heavy
from hauling, lifelines burnished
by soil—we give thanks
for all we'll share, and when the feasting
is through, recite בּוֹרֵא נְפָשׁוֹת *Borei Nefashot*:
                    a blessing for God
                        who *created many souls
                        and their deficiencies.*

Complete, we'd have no reason
to speak, to ask, to reach out

our hands. To seek faces and lives
different than our own.

And here we are, together, mouths full
of words for our hunger and need.

Perfectly imperfect, each of us
is a new way of saying.

לֶךְ-לְךָ

≅

Lech-Lecha

≅

(Go forth)

Mazel Tov

Circular breather, my dog can whine
without ceasing, his tail thumping the wall

beside the bed to call me up and out to the yard
instead. In moonlight, the hydrangeas'

white blossoms are a zodiac of branch-bound
constellations. Once, God called Abraham

out from his tent to the open field to count
the uncountable lights in the sky, promising

offspring bountiful as dust, numerous
as the stars. Like Abraham, I too left

my land, my birthplace, my father's house.
But the closest I have to offspring

is lifting his leg at the azalea, nose busy
with the news the night air brings.

Mazel tov! we say at births and other
joyous occasions, the Jewish go-to

for *Congratulations!* Yet טוֹב *tov* means "good"
and מַזָּל *mazel*, "constellation" or "destiny,"

and sometimes, like Abraham, you must
leave the place that grew you to grow

toward better stars. In the house, my love
is sleeping. Along the fence-top, a procession

of possums reminds that even in darkness
there are those who can see. Above,

trees, thick with summer, frame a porthole
of sky. Maybe, though, it's not always the stars

that matter but the space between them,
the lines we draw to shape the absence,

the lives we forge around what goes missing.
So, if I wish you, *mazel tov*,

know what I'll mean is,
May you live beneath good stars

and find a reason to open
your door to the night.

From the deck, the cool breeze makes a festival
of the silver-lit leaves. Under my palm,

the warmth of his fur, the rise of his ribs.
He doesn't suspect his kidneys

are failing, that his muzzle is white
as the winter the vet has said he will

not live to see. Like all of us, he is
dying; like most of us, he doesn't

know it. His chin on my leg, he trusts me
with the weight of his head.

May the darkness be as much
a blessing as the stars.

Sing, O Barren One, Who Did Not Bear a Child

—Isaiah, 54:1

Her hand sharp in the small of Hagar's back, Sarai, that barren
punster, pimped her handmaid to her husband, saying, "As I am barren

please 'consort' (בנה *bo-na,* in Hebrew) with her" by literally saying,
"I shall be 'built up' (אִבָּנֶה *ibaneh*) through her." A barren

women can still be clever, though rabbis tea-leaved this to imply
a childless woman is a ruined structure in need of rebuilding. Barren,

however, was not a ruin forced on us, but a path my wife and I chose. A choice
not so much against a child as *for* other things—our art, each other: a life barren

only of all we'll never know. God said, "I'll call you
by a different name and your destiny shall change." *Sarai,* barren,

had no children but *Sarah* did. *Mom* is a name I've cried times beyond counting,
yet is a name I'll never be called—less a name than a state of being; once borne,

innate as DNA. "Wife" or "writer," though, are titles non-familial,
vocational, requiring daily upkeep, a renewal of *Yes, I will still bear*

this—and be stronger for it? Who can say. Perhaps we'll end up
most defined by what we are not. Yet bared

by the roof of our ruined structure, we count the countless stars, grow
our shared life in place of bearing

a new one. Because before Sarah and even before Sarai
was the first of the three names she'd eventually bear:

Iscah, whose root might be סָכְתָה *sakhta* (saw) which would make her sight a
    prophet's,

divinely inspired, or סוֹכִין *sokhin*, a duller lot, meaning all "gazed upon" her
beauty: barren

Iscah—precursor to the name Jessica—like all women, torn between being
a seer
and being the one seen. So, prophet, tell me: Is the only happy ending really
a baby?

"Sarai treated [Hagar] harshly, so that she had to flee from her. But
God's messenger found her by a spring of water in the wilderness."
—Genesis 6:6-7

How the Angel Found Her

On the road to Shur, sitting with the bones
of a long-dead ram: one horn at the base
of a juniper, the other in a boulder's
cool shadow.

> (*the child*)

Drydocked in her palm, its skull: a
dumb boat of bone, ferrying nothing
but the rags of its past, the portents
of her future.

> (*the child*
>   *inside her*)

After so many years, death had
no odor; leaning in, though, Hagar
smelled her own sweat, life
                                insisting.

> (*the child inside her*
>   *quickened*)

*"When Abram was ninety-nine years old, God appeared to Abram
and said to him, 'I am יְשַׁי אֶל El Shaddai. Walk in My ways and be
simple and complete.'"*

—Genesis 17:1

And God speaks

like the rattan tap of the cat upflipping

the laundry lid to taffy over and into

the worn clothes, into the scent, spice

and salt of those most loved. O, to be

lulled like that in the rarefied dark. To

surrender to such clement textures, trusting

before thirst or hunger or need domineers,

there will be light and hands to ladle you up,

cradle you safe, ferry you to what follows.

"What woman here is so enamored of her own oppression that she cannot see her heelprint upon another woman's face?"

—*Audre Lorde*

Covenant Between the Pieces

Abram divided

three cows, three goats, three   rams down the middle

and walked with God
between the halves
like a bloody Red Sea.

To cut a deal,   cut animals. Those were literal times.

∞

Say it wasn't just animals.

On one side, Sarah,
his wife,

on the other, Hagar, her
handmaid, his
concubine.

Between them,
a man and jealousy
passed like a flaming torch.

And ahead, for each, a son;
their boys, half-brothers:

Ishmael, whom "God will hear,"
twice-exiled at Sarah's command.

Isaac, whose name, "he laughs,"
seemed more like a taunt with every passing year.

∞

Each woman the other's shadow self:

Sarah, a beloved princess,   as Hagar, a daughter of Pharaoh, had been
in Egypt. Hagar, the fertile body   Sarah had always wanted to be.

∞

Together,
two singular people:

Sarah, the only woman renamed by God; Hagar,
the only woman to give God a name: אֵל רֳאִי *El Roi* (God Who Sees Me).

Together, two wings
are enough to unshackle

from the ground. But, alone, one wing
is just a lonely hand in the distance waving for help.

∞

Because it's often easiest to loathe those most like us,
women often reserve their worst cruelty for each other.

But like neighboring countries, their boundaries
are just agreed-upon fiction.

For Sarah and Hagar, a famine in not just the land but their lives—
especially with women: no friends, no confidantes,
just their husband talking to the empty air
he said was God.

And God didn't
even have a definite name
—bound to Abram was אֵל שַׁדַּי *El Shaddai,*
whose meanings are slippery as that channel through the animals:

"God Almighty"   and also   "The Great Breast"

each integral to the other:

power without care,
a sturdy jug with nothing in it;

                              nurture without action, milk
                                  spilled across a table.

∞

Enough then of God and men
making deals among the carnage.

Let the pieces
form their own covenant, making whole
what others tore asunder.

Let them be
for each other like Eve was
with Adam: עֵזֶר כְּנֶגְדּוֹ *ezer kenegdo—*
עֵזֶר *ezer* (helper)

47

כְּנֶגְדּוֹ *kenegdo*

"compatible with"   and also   "opposite."

No meek helpmeet but   an oppositional helpmate,

strong where you are weak, fit
to take in your flaws. *Partner* in Hebrew
shares the same root as *zygote,* a cell
built from the essence of two people,
the start of a thing intended
to live beyond those
who created it:

a *zug*

ז ו ג

—every mate a kind of mirror
with that selvage
of selves between you.

∞

In the desert where Sarah had banished her, Hagar ran between

two peaks, up and down across land absent of all but her dying son.

On the ground: a woman, terrified, desperate, searching for help.

From afar: with her tracks crisscrossing the sand,

from the Seeing God's-Eye view, Hagar

was a needle mending a great tear. Back and forth,

back and forth, binding two halves, a surgeon suturing a consolable wound.

*During her first banishment, an angel made a covenant with Hagar
for care and countless offspring. Banished a second time, upon
hearing the cries of her son Ishmael, "God opened [Hagar's] eyes
and she saw a well of water. She went and filled the skin with water
and let the boy drink."*

—*Genesis 21:17-19*

And God speaks

a confluence
    of sustenance

        and grace
          in a voice

           substantial
           enough to hold

              like a dowsing rod
                  and seek
             buried metals, hidden

        waters, or, flipped
      inward, the mettle

       to turn and
     brave a fear

   far more easily
avoided.

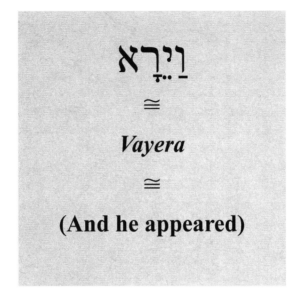

Vayera

≅

(And he appeared)

Will not the Judge of the Earth do justice?

—Genesis 18:25

Rocking, my sister talks, her new son
at her breast, *Did you hear about the mother*
whose kid wandered from the path

in the Everglades? I listen, the room dark,
the carpet soft beneath my back. *The gator came*
out of nowhere. There is the creak

of the chair, the sucking of her son, the rocking
to a rhythm older than them both, until we are all
at the bottom of a spring-fed lake warmed by summer

to thicker than liquid—though all that lurked
were the things most mothers fear: the growing up, growing
away, or, worst, not growing at all. *Before the gator*

could drag him under, she dove and shoved
her arm in its mouth to the shoulder so her son
could wrestle free. Contentment rolls from my sister

in waves, though each crest is slicked with the story's
horror, with the blot of such possible loss. *I understand now,*
she says, *how a woman could do that.* The same

slender moon in the window as the one scything
over Sodom when fire rained down and Lot fled
with his wife, leaving two of their four daughters

trapped in that city. No matter what her husband
said—or even what God commanded—what mother
wouldn't look back and wish that burning hers

instead? And she was not alone: Moses, too,
was met with fire. Both turned to look again: one of them,
the man, became a prophet; the woman, a pillar of salt.

Between her children and the world's hungers: my sister
willing to put her body. Lot's wife unnamed
so she could carry the names of so many. In every field,

on altars of hoof-matted grass, on the rough pulpits
of stumps, a block of salt. A block of salt
facing town: wind-worried, tongue-worn, essential.

שַׁחֲרִית shacharit, whose root is שַׁחַר shachar (dawn), is the traditional Jewish morning prayer service said to have originated with Abraham: "And Abraham rose early in the morning to the place where he had stood before God."

—Genesis 19:27

Learning to Run Barefoot in a Dry Riverbed at Dawn

Cuneiform is also a bone in the foot. Inscribe
your prints beside the birds' and the elks'. Keep time

to the near no-sound of your feet on sand: how
each toe fends and lifts, the different ways the ground

gives. Revise your stride to wend flight-footed
through the riprap at the bends. Pause too long

and horseflies congregate knee-back, neck-side,
wherever blood most hums. And if you fail

to avoid a rock—sharp jut against your sole—
just go to hands and a knee. Before standing, notice

how the new light ribbons east; how eddies
in the sand say this was all once water

and will be again; how,
briefly, there were no words

in your head. And none needed.
Rise. Run. Give thanks for such falter.

"God put Abraham to the test. God said to him, 'Abraham,' and he answered, 'Here I am.'"

—Genesis 21:1

And God Speaks

How it finds you: at attention:
the hair on your forearms, up

the nape of your neck, your whole scalp
prickling. In your ears, the tiny rocks clack

like castanets. All the gates inside you
open: your horses stampede

their pastures, the sky alive with swoop
and dive, a murmuration's quicksilver

shivers. It quivers, the faithful dog
denning your chest . . . There is the keeper's

key in the lock. You are the lock:
every pin aligned, every tumbler turning.

"Absolute faith corrupts as absolutely as absolute power."
—*Eric Hoffer*

Why There Is No Hebrew Word for *Obey*

א.

What came later
was the real trial. Because God knew

Isaac would not die
while Abraham climbed the mountain believing

he would. With conviction
tempered in the fires of his faith,

he walked up, through the shaded valley,
his son, resolute, ahead on the trail; behind them, Sarah—

Isaac's mother, Abraham's wife—a small darkness
in the distance, growing forever

smaller. He bound his beloved son: pulled back
his legs, wrenched back his arms, knotted his ankles to his wrists,

and laid him on that altar like a child falling
through the sky. He held the knife knowing

from every animal he'd ever sacrificed how his son
would jerk and shudder when the blade

opened his throat, the familiar smoke
of offered flesh.

ב.

What came later, even with Isaac alive
in the fields, inside

Abraham was the knowledge
of what he'd been willing to do. When they passed

in the tent, Isaac rubbed a remembered ache
in his shoulder and never again held

his father's eye. Sarah, smelling the imagined
ashes on her husband's fingers, the blood

in the crease of his throat, turned from him
in the night. And on every path Abraham walked

from that day forward, his son as he had been:
a small back barely the span of his hand

slung with the kindling
meant for his burning.

ג.

Seconds from the slaughter
of the one meant to carry his line, of the son

he'd wanted all his life, who's to say
the voice in his head

was God? Judaism is not a faith
but a tradition.

And isn't doubt
the crux of conscience?

Yet what came
later, on a Sabbath morning,

centuries on, was a congregation
in Pittsburgh, reading this story

of Isaac's Binding, of Abraham's
terrible bind, when a man burning

with unquestioning belief
entered with a gun and, with no better angel

to stay his hand, opened fire, believing
the death of Jews would keep our country

safe, believing this massacre—
elderly congregants

bleeding out on the floor—
was God's work.

7.
Who would call such actions
holy? And how many more times

will each of us come down
from the mountain, conviction knocking

like a knife in our belt loop, stained
with all we would have done?

My daily gods
are minor ones: of pride, of lust,

of impatience and complacency.
Yet how many have I harmed

on the way to what I thought
was right—or,

with hindsight, on the way
to what I wanted?

And how many
sorry sacrifices

have I made
of myself?

ה.
What if we turn
from certainty and arm ourselves

instead with questions?
Obey, obey, obey is everywhere

in translation. The real word is
שְׁמַע *shema*: listen.

"If God has chosen me," Isaac replied, "I shall willingly surrender
my soul, but I am gravely concerned about my mother."
                                    —Midrash Tanhuma, Vayera 23

Kaddish for the Living

While Abraham and Isaac were up on the mountain,
Satan dropped by to schrödinger Sarah,

saying her son was dead
but not—

unable to hang on that particular cliff, her heart
plunged over and, before the story's end,

stopped. Stopped
as a perpetual motion machine

given in to its impossibility—
though how we love

the myth of them, how we believe our bodies are,
until they, abruptly, aren't. As the brakes

on my bike, which the mechanic said were
worn to paper, worn out

from working so well for so long. As
my mother's mind.

Like Isaac, my mother is dead
but not: the automatic operations

lost—driving, turning on a stove, following
a plot—while the ingrained etiquette

remains. Lawyer-wife-mother no longer
yet still a sweet shadow in the soundtrack

of every call home. In the Mourner's Kaddish,
death is not mentioned, just praise and petitions

for peace. Though only noon, I tuck her into bed.
And though she breathes beside me,

I am saying goodbye.
There is so much guilt in my grief. But, oh

I mourn her, I mourner, while I still hold her
in my arms. While I fit

my body to hers. Like a cloak. Like a shield.
Like she taught me.

חַיֵּי שָׂרָה

≅

Chayei Sarah

≅

(Life of Sarah)

"After this, Abraham buried Sarah, his wife, in the cave of the field of Machpelah."

—Genesis 23:19

From the Cave, Her Voice

A great man but rarely a good one. A father
to our people, not much of one
to our sons. Greatness, treasured in legends,
is seldom a comfort at the breakfast table.

While I lived, to spot the most distant
caravans, he'd insisted on leaving open
the sides of our tent to welcome every
passing stranger so it could be said

he was the kind who did such things.
Really, though, it was to soothe the silence
that lived between us in the place
of a child. Our world on display,

ready to be detailed chapter and verse.
After me, his life was just summary.

And Abraham came to eulogize Sarah and to weep for her.

—Genesis 23:2

God, she was so beautiful as to be
dangerous, a beacon for all who'd take
my place, who'd take her from me. It was time
that whittled us to these sad bags of sticks.

Yet once, in the lateness of our lives, I knew
again the musk of her hair, the lush ghost
of her young skin. We could have been
any age, any two people unbound

by God's promises. What is long love
if not a reliquary for the selves the other
sheds, a reflecting pool shining back
your shared past, their wishes long-forgotten

flashing bright from the bottom? Even
as we mourn, love gives us back to ourselves.

"With Sarah's death was initiated her eternal life. . . .When some
people die, they leave nothing behind. But after Sarah and Abraham
died, the Jewish people remained."

—Z. Hillel, Itturei Torah

Lemme tell you the one that killed at canasta!

my grandmother says over the phone, laughing,
and all I have to do is close my eyes and I'm there:
the modest brick bungalow on Stanley Lane,
the front patio with its white-pipe
plastic furniture, and in the foyer, a dog,
who for nearly half a century has lifted
its ceramic leg to the same silk plant in an eternity
of staking claim. In the den, matching
orthopedic recliners and, on the fridge,
a plump doll with *Back off, fatso!* emblazoned
on a red leotard washed pink by years
of South Florida sun.

A woman was in the hospital, she begins
with a grin so big I can hear it, *on what she thought*
was the last day of her life, when God visited to say,
"Don't worry, Mrs. Goldberg, you've got many years ahead."

For many years, God visited only Abraham, leaving Sarah
to live on faith alone. My grandfather, too,
was the one who dealt with the powers that be
for their fish market in Jersey City—though
Bernice kept the books, knew every
customer by name, and when the terrified delight
of *Jaws* consumed the country, she was the one
who made a sign for the window: *Get even. Eat fish!*
Yet like Sarah, all promises were conveyed
through her husband, all her covenants secondhand.

Thrilled at God's words, Mrs. Goldberg paid
for the works. Nip, tuck, lift—her butt, her boobs,
her face—she got it all done.

At 95, my grandmother is only five years older
than Sarah eavesdropping on the angels'
gossip of her impending pregnancy, when
she laughed at God and then denied it, when
her withered breasts billowed with milk and
Isaac sprang from her, improbable
as a rabbit from a hat.

But on Mrs. Goldberg's way out of the hospital,
strutting out with her new face and new body, she stepped
from the curb and was mowed down by an ambulance.

"I can't complain," my grandmother says
every time we talk. But she could.
Torn shoulder, bad knee, constant need
to keep an eye on her sugar, so her go-to
cheesecake recipe, as she tells it, is
"Splenda in a blenda'." Nights, she lies alone
remembering gatherings at the lake, rides
on their skiff, the *Miss Sugar*, the boat she'd said
he was "מְשׁוּגָע *meshuga*" to buy, their little dog Troubles.
And though it's been a decade since
his death, she still curses my grandfather
for leaving her to be this lonely.

Finding herself in heaven, Mrs. Goldberg
marched up to God and demanded, "Nu? God, you said
I had a long life ahead. Why am I here?"

While Sarah allowed herself only a chuckle
dusty as a smoker's cough, this far on

in her lineage, my grandmother has outlasted
such propriety. She cracks herself up
before she even gets to the punchline:

God looked her up and down and said, "Mrs. Goldberg?
Sorry, I didn't recognize you."

The way a dust plume announces
a horde on the horizon, her laughter precedes her
and its joy will outlive her—a sonic Dead Sea Scroll,
light from a long-expired star. Whatever the transformations,
when it's Bernice's time, she will be recognized
by her laughter.

Before cellular service, the official designation for voice-grade communication was "Plain Old Telephone Service"

P.O.T.S. Prayer

Blessed art Thou, Lord of the Landline,
whose cables root in the tight-held earth
and stream from pole to pole—tangible

covenants of connection. God of
our fathers, like Abraham,
who declared himself ashes and dust

while bargaining with You in the shade
of his tent. You, who used to be
so accessible, Your number not yet

unlisted, You were obvious
as an antenna. שְׁכִינָה *Shekhinah* of our mothers,
like Sarah, whose womb was a dusty storage room

until her laughter cracked a window
wide enough for a single ray
of life to enter. Of Isaac, unblemished

as a burnt offering, reticent as high noon,
who walked the fields, moving
his lips—no buzz in his pocket

to distract him, no itch to click
a message far from prayer. No, a phone,
like an altar, was a site to approach only

when ready, its cord a means of tethering
you to a place. God of Rebecca, who
leaned over a well and the water rose

to meet her, I too want that force
of connection, with no other demands
patching in. On good days, I can hear

these ancestors breathing, each offering
a new way to pray. Other days, like this day,
when every breath brings another

diversion, the best I can hope for
is some divine dial tone, the stressed/unstressed
hum, reassuring that the line is open,

that when I'm ready, I can make a call.

> *"Until Abraham, people did not grow old. However [because*
> *Abraham and Isaac looked alike] people who saw Abraham said,*
> *'That is Isaac,' and people who saw Isaac said, 'That is Abraham.'*
> *Abraham then prayed to grow old, and this is the meaning [of the*
> *phrase] 'And Abraham was old.'"*
> —Rabbi Jonathan Sacks, on Genesis 24:1

The Question I've Wanted to Hide

What will he do with his body this late
in the day, this crepuscular muscular man?

My father who, at thirty, carried me
when my small legs grew too tired; who,

at fifty—bowlegged, alone, refusing
my help—carried a window AC unit

he'd insisted on buying
up three flights to my first city apartment;

who, at sixty, carried his boat to shore,
rifting a disc. Who, just back

from back surgery, two rods fused to his spine,
made me give chase when he carried

himself to his car while his head
sped on Dilaudid—class-one painkiller,

first-class pain in my neck, so sweet
in his stubbornness. Will he go easy?

Please. Why would he start being easy
now? Or me, with my body, the female

version of his? With the same
massive calves, which flexed in unison,

side by side, as we cycled
from Manhattan to the Canadian border.

For a week, we watched the days change, felt
our legs strengthen. Finally, he delighted

in his daughter taking the lead
and opened a small window

in himself for wonder. And now,
years on, as I've watched him carry

the grief of a wife disappearing
daily, by degrees, as I've watched

his gait stiffen, back hunch, hair thin,
within me, has risen the question

I have to acknowledge: What will I do
when these days exist

in my memory alone, when his body lives
only in our shared carriage,

in the passed-down carry of my stride?

"And Abraham said to his servant . . . 'Put your hand, pray, under my thigh that I might make you swear by the Lord.'"

—Genesis 24:2

Saturday Services at the Provincetown Shore

Just off the parking lot, the lesbians come prepared. Our section
a series of small encampments fortified with tents, coolers,
canvas chairs, and the occasional baby under a pop-up sunshade.
A sunscreen-slathered dealer shuffles cards onto a folding table.

But down a long mechitza of pebbled sand:
the masters of minimalism—men, with little more than flip-flops
and hand towels. Oceanfront anthropologist, trespasser

between tribes, I jog past, note how the sculpted vees of their backs
arrow to an outcropping of asses polished as tumbled stones.
At the shoreline, a man flips into a handstand, penis flapping

like a windsock in low breeze—inverted Michelangelo—until his scan
for admirers unkilters him into the surf. A seagull skims out,
wings slow-clapping the water.

Behind me, the land of women
gripping beer koozies, fanning themselves with hands
of Texas Hold'Em. I'll return, I'm required—all my stuff
is still there. And yes, men can make a bit much of their manhood:

family jewels, third leg, second brain. But the trappings of comfort
can obscure unadorned need. And, for just this barefoot mile,
I let myself envy their economy, the premium they place on desire.

Two by two, men enter
the dunes.

Because anyone taking an oath, said Rashi, *must hold in their hand
a sacred object, and because circumcision was Abraham's first
commandment and came to him through suffering and was beloved*

to him, he chose it as the object on which his servant swore. For these moments
they share, no matter what Leviticus says, pursing tight its prurient verses,
these men, too, are taking a kind of oath: Our bodies are all we entail.

"Isaac went out to לָשׂוּחַ in the field before evening" (Genesis 24:63).
Lasu'ach is a verb that holds both talking and listening and can be
translated as "pray," "meditate," or "converse" with God.

Ordinary Immanence

In New York, sidewalks were so crowded it was easier
to walk in the street, and three stories up
from all the elbows and breath, always
the same city dream: in the back
     of my cramped apartment, a door
I'd somehow not seen. I'd press my ear to it
and hear the cavernous echo
of air arcing through hidden, innumerable rooms,
     rooms I owned but had never entered.

Many years, many states away, in a far
     more spacious place, at the braking
of a garbage truck, at the creak and hoist
of its mechanical arm pinioning a block's-length
     of bins to hoist and dump, I look up
from a book and know (the truck outside
rumbling away, my waste fraternizing with the waste
     of my neighbors) that I want
to believe in God. Just like that—a new door
in a room I thought I knew by heart.

My hand is on the doorknob now, my ear
to the grain.

     But what I hear
        is the crackling hum
           of light bulbs above, the tissued whisper
     of an iris opening, the deep breathing

of the daily world—nothing
from the other side.

How do you listen for a sound you've never heard?
Or, more precisely,
for a sound you know so well
you've never heard it?

At First Sight, Many Seeings Later

Lifting my chin, my wife said, *When you look*
at my breasts like that, you make my face
feel lonely. So this was new marriage ·

on a Wednesday morning. When
Rebecca saw Isaac the first time, he was striding
the noon field. A man at full sunlight, he cast

no shadow. From her camel, most translators
spin נָפַל *naphal* into "alighted," allowing her
some dignity. The truth is it means she fell:

in a cloud of desert dust, Rebecca was a smitten,
resplendent heap lanterning up at her future
mate. The truth is, in the beginning, her face

was too much for me. The force of my desire,
matched. Now, years on, we have matching
slippers and each night, on the couch, between us

the dog snores. How little we look
at what we think we know, less seeing
than simply noting, *Yes, still there.*

Yet if the past of love is longing,
the future, grief—at least for one of us—
let the present praise

the little brown bird of the familiar. This swift
flown into the sweet sheet of her skin:
wings in upstroke: the apexed angles

of her collarbone. Let me fall
from my camel again and again.
Let me gaze up and see her new.

תּוֹלְדֹת

≅

Toldot

≅

(Begettings)

And God said to Rebecca, "Two nations are in your womb, and two
peoples from within you shall be divided; the one shall be stronger
than the other, the older shall serve the younger."

—Genesis 25:23

The Bravest of the Birds

Through the gauzy curtain, our parents
were a flicker of television in the darkened room,
which made me the only witness
           as my sister wrote her best self in the air.

From the balcony of a beachside hotel, our bare feet
pitted by concrete, she called to the circling gulls.
She was hungry but loved those birds enough
to empty her bag of breakfast rolls, hard opening
to soft in her hands. Unable to fling through the bars,
I helped her onto a white plastic chair and, suddenly
taller than me, the rhythm of her throws
drew birds until they stretched for stories
above and below, until the hollow beating of
their wings thundered the blue afternoon and my heart
clutched and fell with each of them—
the controlled violence of their hurtling dives,
their effortless rise—while she just leaned out,
past the toprail, past safety or sense, trusting herself
to the sky, answering their cries with her operatic own:
           this lofty whirling winged wheel
                     resting entirely
                on the fulcrum of my sister.

The idea of luck—or its lack—the question
of joy, and who knows it, haunts me.

Sometimes we go months without speaking.
Anger and envy close as two sisters pressed
to the same rail. When she hurts me most, I try to breathe
again that salt-warmed air. To see her
face incandescent in the sunlight, her hair so bright
it looked like fire, the bravest of the birds
arcing in, taking bread directly from her hand.

In the village of my body, two people

vie for the throne, box-sprung and
gold-leafed though it is. The firstborn
is lusty, muscled, veins cantillating
with sunheat, field and flesh, she is all
hunger—for a mess of stew, for
a burger, she'd give anything, even
her birthright, that divine protection
that those who curse her are cursed
and those who bless her get
God's *attaboy*, God's divine
pat on the back. The second is hermetic,
blanched as a leek and wilting
at her texts, a root vegetable plucked
from darkness into darkness,
immaculate poet of the tents.
The small Solomon in my gut
notes how each runs
on the same clean-burning will,
which in a mortal body
is like pure light
through a dirty window: it spatters
particular shadows. And of what worth
is such a birthright anyway? What
would it mean if one part of myself—
vigor to the point of violence,
or giving to the point
of giving in—if one were blessed

beyond the other, granted
license to govern and multiply?
My belly growls, small Solomon
whispers, *It feels better to be kind
than right*. In a clearing
between my ribs, I plant
a shade tree—ideal spot for treaties—
and hope it grows to block the two
rusting water towers of my village's
warring sides: one tagged
MIGHT MAKES RIGHT, the other
airbrushed *the meek shall inherit*.
The tree will wait there, bannering
its leaves, until my two women
can agree to dig one well from which
both will draw: *balance*, etched on one
side; on the other, *integration*.

Comfort Food

Every morning of my first year, my mother's father
drove over at dawn to bathe me and walk with me among trees,
touching my tiny fingers to things as he named them,
saying, *bark*, saying, *web*, saying, *air* and *grandfather* and
granddaughter, all to say, *Welcome; I have waited
so long for you.* At a family dinner, he fed me
berries, my first solid food. When he whistled,
I pressed my nose to his nose, eyes shut

tight as my grandmother's were, years later, against
those many mourners clutching hors d'oeuvres uneaten,
barbed with toothpicks, crowding her
home. They spoke relentlessly of this man she'd loved
for half a century, whose side of the bed
was suddenly cold. My arm around her shoulders,
we rocked to a dirge only she heard, a growing gale
that broke from her in a cry without bottom or sides, a keening

that now lives in me alone, along with the grapple
of her lungs, years later, in those last days
as I rubbed lotion onto her bone-latticed back,
eased water through her lips, the rend of each breath
as she begged us to help her go, and, now, the consuming
remorse that I couldn't, that I hadn't, done what she asked.

At his grandfather Abraham's death, Jacob made a simple stew
to comfort his father. Lentils, the Talmud said, because
they're round as the wheel of mourning that touches
each of us in turn; lentils, because they have
no seam as a mourner has no mouth,
silenced as we are by sorrow.

In the middle of my life, as I cook, I hum—that close-mouthed,
compromised song—lamentation the only tune
I can carry. Death: the creation story
in reverse, blood becoming earth, red lentils mulching
to brown in the pot.

At the counter, I stand and eat: yielding as wet soil, heavy
as grief, a stubborn grain between the teeth: nothing
to bite down on, filling all the same. To my dead,
I sing, *I have waited so long for you.*

"And God appeared to [Isaac] and said, 'Do not go down to Egypt; continue to dwell in the land of which I've told you, sojourn in this land, and I will be with you and will give you blessing . . .'"
—Genesis 26:2-3

And God speaks

in a blaze of autumn:
loud fleets of geese,

pirouetting maple keys,
a rain of gold

from the gingkoes;
squirrels, fall's fat acrobats

gnawing husks
in the boughs of the walnut

before rustling up
the dusty cinnamon

of downed leaves.
The passing hours

pares trees
to their elegant bones.

Everything conspiring
to make space and time

palpable: God, an indwelt
clearing to dwell in.

"And Isaac dug anew the wells dug by his father Abraham."
—*Genesis 26:18*

Joint Account

Mother is brushing her teeth
while on the toilet again.
She'd done the calculations: 24 hours
saved this way each year. Next,
the home gym, 60 minutes on a bike
going nowhere. Then oatmeal
sprinkled with chemicals
approximating sweetness,
followed by a soda (diet)—calories
something to eat, not drink. With such care

she kept the books and her figure,
kept the household schedule.
And as soon as I could sign
on the waiting line, she took me
to the local bank and opened
an account in both our names.

In the mornings now, no matter
the weather, I leave
my love in our warm bed
to get my miles in. Run on no breakfast,
listing off the tasks ahead,
aiming for economy
of minutes and miles.

And now that numbers come to my mother
slowly, when in five minutes
she asks the same question three times,

I wish I could ask: Was it worth it?
What is the value of desire denied?
Where did you hoard all that stored time?

For what am I saving mine?

If you can't remember, Mom,
I'll drive us to that old bank,
give you my card, my pin.
Finally, please, cash in; please, cash in.

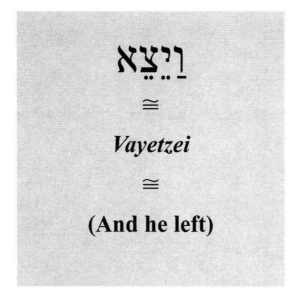

וַיֵּצֵא

≅

Vayetzei

≅

(And he left)

> *"To go in the dark with a light is to know the light.*
> *To know the dark, go dark."*
>
> *—Wendell Berry*

And I, i did not know it.

While galaxies surged and flared above, Jacob
saw only what needed to be done—he smoothed
his bedroll, tidied his sandals, all the small things

before sleep—his lamp's glow a shield
against the unfathomable dark. When he
lay back, though, despair slid over him

like a stone so heavy it would take
three men to shoulder it from the mouth of the well.
Yet as smoke spiraled from the candle's wick,

patient stars lustered up like a forest of quaking,
luminous leaves, like fluorescent reefs
in the deepest sea, and the earth tipped, plunging

him into sky; angels scaled the ladder
of his spine; his body hollowed, a conduit
for the divine. Waking, he saw what had been

there all along—quartz veining the stone
beneath his head, the tear in his bedroll
darned by his mother, how his sandals

held the press of his soles; he saw
the site holy and said, *God is in this place*
and I, i did not know it. But why the double

I, the nervous stutter? In that moment of sight,
it was not God but himself he'd unnoticed—
freeing him, for an instant, from the self's hold.

Even our feeble flames enough
to divert us from seeing,
so we access the divine

by unknowing the I,
taking us back to ourselves, fully,
for the first time.

מַעֲרִיב ma'ariv *is the traditional Jewish evening prayer said to have originated with Jacob. Avivah Zornberg wrote, "Jacob is, in fact, the first human being [in the Torah] to pray in the dark. . . . Darkness, too, is a way of knowing God."*

Prayers from a Dark Room

א. *Gehenna*

If Hell is less fiery furnace
than a mirrored room

with all the lights
left on, with nowhere to hide

that what burns
is within us—all the guilt

and sorrow from
which we now can't look

away, then let us
accept our faces

as they are. Let us remember
that one word,

דּוֹלֶקֶת *doleket*, means both
"in flames" and "full of light"

and know our pain
can be a source of sight.

ב.   *I am afraid to own a Body—I am afraid to own a Soul—*

In Eden, garments of light sufficed, each human a lantern
lit from within, inextricable

from their ignition—but now, banished,
this dim skin suit, by which the spirit is dusked

to firefly: such faint flares, such cold glow. Lonely lighthouses,
each of us. We blink, we beacon, we long to chorus, we wait

for a blaze in return, until—*there!*—allied, we pulse one
to the next; bind in divine

synchrony: for a moment, the whole
planet a field of fallen stars. And from this ensemble

bonfire, like smoke scorching from the narrows
of a throat, our fears. A cry

for not ownership but communion, a cry to be answered
with expanse
     of air, of wind, of רוּחַ *ruach,* that godbreath,

gentling in toward every torn thing, its breach
however meager—moving leaf into leaves, melding

body to soul, making of every opening a mouth and
setting us all to singing. Can you hear it?

A torch song for the kindred world, this fleeting one
         we're searching for.

ג.   *Prayer for the Word Made Light*

Bathe the window within us
in photo-sensitive silver. Let us

aperture. Let us dilate. What lasts
is what is found

by light. Negatives of the divine,
let us enter the stop bath

of the ordinary world. Where
we are most vulnerable, most

exposed, that's what makes
the print. We become

what is burned into us: what
we open ourselves to.

Another Calling

Alone in the shallows of a spring-fed inlet,
I was a child who believed in nothing
but experience. Arms out, swaying
in the currents, a submerged log
was my balance beam—toes digging for purchase
along its silt and coarse ridges—until the log
opened its mouth, revealing
long, blunt teeth. Not bark but scales
beneath my feet, not swimming so much as levitating
to shore. Driven up the slippery wooden stairs,
up out of myself by terror, over the rough lip
of the retaining wall and onto the grass,
where I finally dropped
back into my body, knowing myself just a little
better for that time away.

Does it matter if it's true
or not—a child's phantasm or really
happened?

        After Jacob's first prophetic
dream, inside him was the young man
who once saw a sky filled with angels on ladders,
who woke into a new knowing of God
and cried out,

מַה־נּוֹרָא הַמָּקוֹם הַזֶּה

Ma norah ha'makom hazeh!
(How fearsome is this place*!*)

Of God's many names, one is הַמָּקוֹם *Ha'Makom*
(The Place): the One Who is the World but Whom the World

Cannot Contain. And maybe Jacob gave us
another name, had truly meant,

                 Fear *is* The Place.

            Inside me, the girl who'd balanced
on the back of a gator and lived
to remember it. Who'd returned the following week
to that same water, which was cold and clear
as air in winter:
               paddling up, plummeting down,
it was a city of swimmers on invisible ladders, and I dove
past them into the spring rising from the dark
karst cavern, swam into the narrow parting
of those walls, a slot just wide enough
for one, down into the hissing, bubbling cascade,
the torrent strengthening the closer I came, afraid
but still swimming, toward the upwelling source.

Fear one more facet of God, the flare
of what's worth noticing.

So Jacob served seven years for Rachel and they seemed to him but a few days because of his love for her.

And he *watered* her flock and *kissed* her mouth,
וַיַּשְׁקְ *wayashq* and וַיִּשַּׁק *wayishaq*, binding care with the carnal,
their muzzles warm beneath his tending hands,
her mouth bright as the nectar of pomegranates.

Desideratum is a word for something wanted
or needed, whose root means both
"to find a lack of" and "to miss," binding
the discovery of an absence
         with the already active longing for it:
         our greatest needs indwelt within us
long before we begin to name them.
The lack of you

alive in me long before
I knew your face.

"And Jacob swore by the Fear of his father Isaac."

—Genesis 31:53

Personal Injury Parents

Before every county fair, they brandished the damages
from last year's lawsuits, cautioning with such passion
that later, as moths threw themselves at the lesser moons
strung along the fairway, on a night flushed
sweet with the grease of funnel cakes, with the bass
pulsing cheap speakers and the heat of a whole town's
teenage anticipation, instead of thrilling
to the moment the girl from math class
got so scared on the Gravitron she grabbed my hand
and held it, my head swam with the tally of teeth
lost to sudden stops, the number of fingers
severed. *Don't you know what could happen?*
How many ways the world had to hurt me.

∞

Back in the days when muscling a massive rock
from atop a well was the closest thing going
to a strongman game, Jacob met his love Rachel
and wept. Sages say he foresaw her early death.
But who thinks of death at the very moment
their new life begins?

On a lonely mountain, as sunlight caught the knife
raised above his father Isaac's neck, the eyes of his grandfather
were still scorched from seeing Sodom consumed to ash,
from witnessing what happens when we don't do
what God asks, and Abraham's tears fell from his eyes

to Isaac's; tears that decades later dimmed Isaac's sight
as he announced to his sons his imminent death—

in a masterstroke of Jewish guilt—fifty years
before he actually died: all those burnings searing up
in Jacob's throat in that moment of first meeting.

∞

My mother's college roommate took
her own life; my father, raised in a world
cruel to women, has three daughters. She said
it made her afraid of feeling too much;
he grasped too hard, wincing as we aged
past the protection of his arms.

∞

Death meditations of our forefathers, pain
of our parents winding our genes tight as wisteria,
reaching, always reaching for another part of us
to bind to, whispering out when we least expect it.
All winter long I misremember Roethke (*I learn by fearing
where I have to go*) and can't let my beloveds leave
without saying, *I love you. Be careful. Don't die.*

∞

Separate from damaged property, "personal" is an injury
to the body, mind, or spirit. My given parental counsel—
unhired, unfireable, their undisclosed hourly rate
accruing for an unnamed future date—were so focused
on suffering, they never mentioned the fear that brings us
closer, that whinnies up from your knees
to lean you against the one you love, or how trembling
sets you in harmony with the elemental
strands of all matter.

As that creaking, poorly-rigged
contraption spun us into the dark air, the neon

Tilt-a-Whirl screaming below, there was that girl's
scared sacred hand, hot in mine. Our whole lives
a fairway lined with dicey enticements,
with joy for those willing to chance a ride.

Measure for Measure

Was it my parents' sour grapes that have set
my teeth on edge? Or is this bitterness
from seeds I've sown myself?

The woman I left
weeping in an East Village restaurant.
The one I had to wrestle back

from a seaside cliff, an empty fifth
of Maker's in her fist. Calls unmade. Letters
unsent. Sundered friendships

left to founder. I want to say
I'm always trying, always learning
from my mistakes. But my thoughtfulness stalls

so often at intention. My fault or fate's?
And which is worse: to be guilty or powerless?

∞

Because he wanted nothing more than
his father's hand on his head, Jacob pretended
to be his hairy brother, sheathing his smooth arms

in the skin of a goat so freshly slaughtered
its blood pooled in the crook
of his elbow. But it burned,

that stolen blessing, guilt making him a mark
for others: The uncle who stole his labor,
stole the wrong sister into his bed—

and with her true face revealed by morning,
this sister who, from the blood-stained sheets,
defended herself with Jacob's own actions,

There is no teacher without a student;
I kept your lesson in mind.

An eye for an eye, a tooth for a tooth.
What else could he do but bow his head?
Her deception was heavy with the scent of home.

∞

Or is it more an eye for a tooth?
A tooth for a tumor? A stray bullet
entering a blameless window. A virus,

aimless, targeting none and all. Yet
if we are not at fault for our tragedies,
can we own our triumphs? Own

anything? Her promotion, his star turn—
ours, or the choice vintage of our parents'
vineyards, a particular alignment

of the stars? Does anything happen
for a reason? *An eye for an eye*
makes the whole world blind, Gandhi

might or might not have said. And, yes,
providence annuls agency but it also provides
a pattern, a Dungeon Master to petition

and please: Do *X*, don't do *Y,* claim
you're in control though you flare
your face to the sky, hoping to game
the system. Randomness is hard to bear.

וַיִּשְׁלַח

≅

Vayishlach

≅

(And he sent)

The Hendiadys of Marriage

As "milk and honey" signals abundance,
"image and likeness" that we are
chips off God's block, with its love
of hendiadys (one thing by means of two)
the Torah advises, why use one word
                        when two will do better?

∞

Jacob was hendiadys par excellence.
Crooked heel-sneak, willing
to scam a blind old man, he was also
Israel, able to wrestle from God
the blessing of a true name.

Surely as Jacob married Rachel and
her sister, Rachel married
both those men.

∞

And aren't each of us who are married
married to at least two people: the one
we knew, we thought, who drew us;
the one who emerges those times
we say, *Oh, you're not yourself today—*
a gentle chiding that *the person I married*
wouldn't act this way; and maybe too

the one who delights you by knowing
every bird on your walk by song alone.

∞

Despite being a mother of monotheism,
Rachel loved the household gods
enough to steal them from her father.
צָרָה *tzarah*, one Midrash calls them, another
name for "rival wife."

∞

Which is the true partner and which the rival?
Who they are now or the version they'll strive for?
The one we wanted, or the one we have,
or the potential one just waiting up ahead
whom neither of you can quite imagine?

∞

Before we married, my wife
had never hiked—the woods a specter
of constant danger. But now
she strolls the trails with ease,
pointing out uncanny eruptions
of ghost pipe, the pom-pommed
exuberance of mountain angelica.

Marriage is a mutual View-Master:
        two images at once
necessary for depth of vision, which is itself
a trick of the eye: that woman, confident
in the woods, able to name what she sees,

or that girl sure she'll lose herself
among the trees—
                The multitudes
we each contain. The illusion of one
when all remain.

"[Rachel said to Jacob], 'Here is my maid Bilhah. Consort with her, that she may bear on my knees and that through her I too may have children.'"

—Genesis 30:3

"When Leah saw she had stopped bearing children, she took her maid Zilpah and gave her to Jacob as concubine."

—Genesis 30:9

No one's loves, no one's wives

we were just kitchens: four hands
to make his meals, two ovens to make
his sons. Unlike those bickering sisters,
at least we had each other. In the list
of matriarchs, our names are scribed
in lemon juice. To see them,
you must hold that text to the fire.

How Many More

Like a griffin born from a lion
and an eagle, like the Leviathan coiling

the world's watery root, the daughters
of Jacob: mystical creatures or just bad

translations? Or were they like aurochs—real
animals now mythic, hunted into extinction?

While the men and their mothers
walked travel-worn paths,

their twins murmured along animal runs
rutted by hoof and claw, piled

with scat. Like the bars
of a cell, they white-knuckled the lines

they were hidden behind: so many women
left uncounted, unnamed. And how many more

made extinct by men's hungers? Yet they went on
carrying babies, comforting brothers and husbands,

hanging laundry that snapped like flags
in the breeze, bearing the standard

of their whispered nation. Like modern women
who typed and revised their husbands'

nascent notes into novels and speeches,
lifting the words from serviceable

to sublime, like the uncredited scientists
and inventors—stepping stones

to the men who claimed the fame
that came from their efforts. Hazy figures at the edge

of dreams, if only they'd taken
their father's story of wrestling the angel

until dawn as their own, had taken their men
in a grappler's embrace

steady as a winepress, extracting the names
not given, the birthrights denied.

They were the leaders of the true lost tribes.

"And Jacob called the name of the place Peniel: for I have seen God face to face, and my life is preserved."

—Genesis 32:30

And God Speaks

אִישׁוֹן *ishon—*
Hebrew for the open gate at the center
of our eyes, which most translators cultivate
into *apple*; in plain English, *pupil*, from the Latin for *girl* and *boy—*
closer to the literal   meaning: *little man.*

For when standing near   enough to another, face
to face—diligent pupil, learning all you can; apple of their eye,
cherished above all others—you can see yourself
reflected and held, and know your own eye
holds them too.

Godwrestling

The river has tasted the salt of your skin, has lapped
at your calves with its current. The river has swallowed

the press of your steps. There is no record of your crossing.
The river is between you and everything you call your life.

So you step into a stranger's arms. Your shoulder fits
theirs like a bone in its socket, their jaw notches yours.

All around you, a profusion of oleanders
beams back the moonlight, offering a carpet of fallen petals.

In your arms, all the promises you've yet to keep, all
you've done that shames you. But what is wrestling

if not an embrace? It's too dark to see
you have the same face and only like this, cheek to cheek,

each looking over the other's shoulder, can you see
the world whole. Close, at first, as a slow dance,

you spin and spin, your tracks a tight coin; matched,
you step out, making a spear tip of your bodies; matched,

you step further, levered like rafters, needing the other
to stay aloft—your tracks trace widening circles, ringing

out through the fallen blossoms. Names are required
only when not alone. This stranger

does not give you a new name, just dippers up
the true one you tender in your chest. The day is breaking

the night's hold; the far bank is calling.
On one side, you. On the other, your life. Join them.

"There is no one who has not their hour and no thing that has not its place."
—*Pirkei Avot 4:3*

Perseverance Prayer

Be it rug or couch or bed, the dog
can't help but turn and turn and turn again
before lying down, his angle always

a little off, the vantage never quite
as desired. Still the ritual persists.
Yet once in a prairie gone tall

with summer, high grass whispering
with afternoon breeze, he began—one, two,
three times around—and the stalks found

new joints with each of his orbits, swaying,
kneeling, prostrating away from him
into a massive golden wreath, an ideal bed.

Pursuits others call pointless are often just
right actions in need of their right moment.

*"The sons of Jacob came upon [the men they had] slain and
plundered the city because [those men] had defiled their sister."*
—Genesis 34:27

And Her Name Meant Everything
from Judgment and Strife to Vindication

I know reason, I know rationalize, can
adage how *hurt people hurt people* and cite
the ancient laws of a woman's fault
for her own poor fortune, trace their echoes
back through my wife to her mama's
mama in Kentucky, tucking a twenty
in her grandbaby's bra, just in case,
warning her away from the woods
with the double-edged words, *Now, don't you go
and get yourself raped.* And still, Dinah,

I understand your brothers' fury, their willingness
to strike down a whole damn town
if it would make you feel even a little
bit better. When I think of you, silenced,
freighted with your complicated name,
your savage fate; when I think of
her, the woman I love, of all
the women wounded simply because a man could
not stop himself, of all the women
shamed for the actions of others,
my stomach furnaces a brimstone
and fire I wish hot enough to rain
through time and raze all that damage
gone with a lick of blue-backed flame.

I tell myself, I do, if she's found
a way to forgiveness I should too.

But the so many days I kiss salt
from her eyes. The startle if I take her too swiftly
in my arms. A pack of coyotes
quickens my veins, keens its need
to hunt anyone who hurt her, even
the dead, and leave nothing
but twists of hair, bits of bone.
For those I love, my love comes
with this catch.

       My most devouring fury,
though, is for me. For no matter how I protect
every day forward, there is the past—
unchangeable, indefensible. Which makes
such anger just sorrow with armor on.

After the massacre carried out by his sons in Shechem, God orders
Jacob to build an altar in Bethel. "As they set out, a terror from God
fell on the nearby cities, so that they did not pursue the sons of Jacob."
                                                    —Genesis 35:1-7

And God Speaks

Is there fear when it happens?
That collapses your shoulders

like the closures of a cape, that bows
your head until you cease

to see? Or is it
electrical surge

with you as conductor, the wings
of your scapula yearning

toward each other, head thrown back,
arms out, hands flexed wide? Your whole

body arched and open—a conduit,
a tuning fork. Not terror but

awe—fear with a hinge
toward entrance:

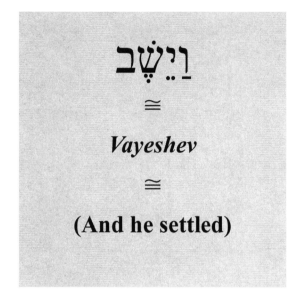

≅

Vayeshev

≅

(And he settled)

Avivah Zornberg notes וַיֵּשֶׁב יַעֲקֹב *Vayeshev Yaakov (And Jacob settled)—the first words of this parshah—point to Jacob's desire for* יִשּׁוּב הַדַּעַת *yishuv ha-da'at (a settled mind), as opposed to* טֵירוּף הַדַּעַת *tiruf ha-da'at (a torn mind).*

Torn Mind

A rabbit savaged in the field, my mind
is that torn, that scattered.
All dog-paddle day, all surface
and screens, I sink sometimes
but bob back up.
Someone, somewhere
needs an answer.
Not bold enough to run from destiny,
I let it seep from me instead.

So though he shivered in the briny dark,
krill wreathing his ankles, I find
I am jealous of Jonah.

Like Nineveh, I am a city in need of saving.
Like Jonah, I have words stuck
in the scrim of my ribs
and the whale seems
an ideal retreat—
three days, three nights
at a depth I can barely imagine.

The whale, both vessel and message:
to settle into time like it does
into water. To patient

beside the rumbling pump room

of the heart. The quiet there
like God—nowhere and everywhere
at once. The holiness of that
wholeness. Of what rises to meet it.

"Hear this dream which I have dreamed."

—Genesis 37:6

Dream in Which I Give You My Memories as Dreams
for Frannie, at four months

Even in sleep you hunger: purse your lips and bellow
your cheeks as though to nurse from the world.
Material things, you'll outgrow too quickly;

so here are the summer afternoons
of my childhood, with their endless horizons
and fast-passing storms. Here's reading in the branches

of a pine tree, sap leopard-spotting the soles of your feet.
Here is your small hand in a large tank while stingrays
circle below. With each pass, they ripple

up to the steady press of your palm, choosing you
again and again. Here, too, is a theatre
dug into the limestone bank of a natural spring.

In the dim and dank, kids snack from plastic treasure chests
while parents check their phones. But then,
through a curtain of bubbles,

mermaids appear, smiles bright
as their nylon tails, indelible as their waterproof rouge.
    A little girl leaps up, gripping

a seat on either side of the aisle as though to keep
from flinging herself at the glass. Her parents look down,
mutter, *Sorry, she's always like that.*

Women, finned and sequined, hair waving in the water,
pirouette and flip and sip air from a hose,
                    and joy rises in the girl

                until she cannot help but prow her body forward
far as her arms allow and scream,
                    MERMAIDS, I LOVE YOU!

Like that. May you always be like that. Loving
with such abiding, improbable abandon. And may life,
like a long muscle of light, lift through the waters to find you.

When He Was Not

When brown froth scummed a cistern's
surface, villagers threw in clods of earth,
believing—dirt on dirt—they'd sink the rot
to the bottom. Joseph's brothers threw in
Joseph, into a dry pit scuttling
with scorpions and snakes. Miracle
he didn't break every bone, though
his perfect curls were mussed. Maybe
it was a joke, a wet willy in the ear, rope burn
on the wrist, big-brother kind of a lesson.
He rehearsed how he'd tell on them
to their father. But their words fell
like dirt as he lay in the dim and listened:
Pretty boy. Tattletale. Conceited
dreamer. In the middle of summer,
a winter solstice: the shortest
day, the longest night. They'd stolen
his coat. He shivered. Who knows how long
he'd been down there.
                        In the hours, the weeks
to come, one brother would cry, *The boy is not here!*
And his father would weep, *Joseph is torn apart,*
savaged by a beast built in his father's
own mind. But for now, a cloud blocked
the light like God's sight pressed to the eyepiece
of a microscope. Splayed as a specimen,
Joseph was rendered by that looking. For
the first time he knew לְהִתְפַּלֵל *le'hitpalel* (to pray)
is reflexive, meaning an action done
to oneself, literally *to judge yourself.*
Rot-sunk, abandoned, for a long
breath, he was not, he was torn
apart, before reseeing himself in God's

vision. And for the rest of his life,
he was a man putting himself
back together. A man with this pit
inside him, with the knowledge
that everyone he met carried
a similar cistern: an emptiness
that doubles as a reservoir.

Wake, you sleepers from your sleep!

—Maimonides, on the message of the shofar blasts each Jewish New Year

Are creatures' only value the sounds
we make through them? How their hides
hide and protect us? How their blood
greases the clanking wheel of our plots,

easing our narratives forward?
It is their skin on which our stories
are written. You, sons who flayed the coat
from your brother, the skin from a goat,

who dipped the first in the blood of the second
to fleece your father
into thinking Joseph savaged by an animal,
when the only animals there were you—

listen past the blasts to their source.
Your smooth-skinned father Jacob,
who slaughtered a goat to impersonate
his hairy brother, wearing its skin

to fool your blind grandfather
over a shared dish of its flesh. His father
Isaac, begat by Abraham
who pulled a last-minute ram from the thicket

to slaughter in Isaac's stead: a surrogate son
bound and slit-throated on the altar. From that ram,
the sinews that strung David's harp, the skin
that gird the loins of Elijah, the horns sheared off

and hollowed, hallowed into sacred instruments
used to mark a new moon, a new battle, the start
of a new year, which marks the battle
with ourselves, ten days of trembling repentance.

The ritual wail that forces us back
to Abraham's wind-raked mountain,
the looming knife, the moment of choosing
which life to end, which power to serve, and maybe

even earlier, when we could have chosen
not to be there at all. Look outside yourself.
Even now, a flock of shofars grazes the field.
Their lips parse the tangled browse:

listen: the soft separation
of stalks from the dirt, the green
grind of their teeth. Each living thing
is its own call to attention.

מִקֵּץ

≅

Miketz

≅

(At the end of)

And who are you supposed to be?

asked of every monster, hero, and outlaw
with a pillowcase or orange plastic pumpkin,

as they take their star turn, porch-lit centerstage. This
is my love's favorite holiday. The rest of the year, identities

in which we have little say. And so many of us betrayed
by our off-the-rack bodies and how we're made

to cover them. *And who are you?* Not this, this
is not me. The so-many answers the eye can't see.

∞

One story says in Eden we were clothed
in light and only after

were stoppered in this skin. Who were we
supposed to be: these dim husks or human lanterns?

Once a knock-kneed girl in knockoff clothes,
she wields fashion as passport, armor, play.

Forced into dresses for synagogue when I was still itchy
with the fit of "girl," I favor function and feel: shirts worn

to cotton cobwebs, ballcaps with brims split as baclava,
I wear my clothes until I might molt them and finally step light.

∞

Like our souls wear speech and action to be known
in this fallen world, the Torah wears stories

that look like us: Joseph in his many-colored coat
was known for how he was dressed

by others, so his clothes bore only false witness. Yet even
these mistakes were a privilege. For everyone else, one size

fit all: prayer shawl as garment, bedsheet, burial shroud.
In Hebrew, בֶּגֶד *beged*—"clothing" and "betrayal," the same word.

∞

Even now, October trees cling to their summer leaves, blazing
with the effort, turning every mountain trail to fiery tunnel,

the expanse beyond curtained off. Only in the bareness
of winter can we finally see. But how long can we stand it,

that shivering vision? With her seasonal wardrobes—
embroidered sundresses giving way to well-cut coats—

she has taught me how every mode of seeming
has its season. And some days, I run so many miles

I slip my own traces and can leave, for a moment, that assembled self
behind. And some nights, the moon slips its coat of clouds to find

our window. *Who are you?* I am this body you've chosen
for your arms. *And who are you supposed to be?*

I am, we are. Clothed in nothing
but these bodies, through our bodies, we get beyond our bodies.

How Long Before

To move in the wet heat of Florida summer is to be carried
in the mouth of an animal. But inside my parents' house,
kept chill as a mausoleum, my mother paces and weeps

in a ragged nightgown she refuses to change, her hands
two anxious dishcloths trying to wring themselves dry.
Because I am not the person I'd like to be, I shut the door

on this, on my father's poor job of pretending
not to cry, and, between fences draped in air potato vines
beetle-eaten to a path of tattered valentines, run

as though I could leave any of this behind. As Joseph tried to
when he named his first son מְנַשֶּׁה *Manasseh* (He-Who-Makes-
Forgetting), a word that hints at memory evaporating

like water from a sizzling street, that heat
hungry as the silverfish swimming
my childhood books, leaving holes in all the old stories.

But to name someone after what you say you've forgotten
is to make of them a neon arrow to the relentless past,
one you'll someday return to. This is not that.

The mother I've lost is lost for good. The only cure
for such decay is its completion, when she's forgotten
even forgetting. In the mountains I've made my home,

vine barrens of kudzu, invasive as her illness, mask
every gall, burl, and blight. So come, high-climber,
you foot-a-night-vine. May all her buried memories remain

for her unmarked, unnamed. Cover it all
with your nullifying green, be a sea that waives over everything.
And if it brings her peace, let her forget even me.

"Joseph recognized his brothers, but they did not recognize him."
—*Genesis 42:8*

Sibling Beit Midrash

Cave crickets pulse the walls of the shed while mice
scurry the baseboards and there, beside slumped
bags of potting soil . . . there in attics,
whose rafters are woven with webs, whose boards
sag with boxes long forgotten and boxes
hauled down for some annual reason . . . there
in basements dank with the slow seep
of groundwater . . . there in the dusty closets
of memory are the sacred scrolls
of our childhood. Released from their grotty arks,

we unroll them across the kitchen table. My sisters and I
lean close, coffee and crumbs anointing the pages,
pointing and laughing and reading aloud, and—
as we are also both siblings and Jews—arguing.
Who wrote this?! one says. *That's not how it was!*
There's so much left out, another complains.

So go the days of Sibling Beit Midrash.

Despite the singular lives we've built
with other people, in other places, to each other
we're always the younger model
we were by circumstance and birth,
before our self-made updates.

Yet just as when looking in a mirror, you notice
not the glass and its cut but the momentary *you*
it reflects, when revisiting the shared scrolls

of our past, our readings reveal more
about the teller than the text—a text that reads us
as we read it. Only they understand

how, even now, in need of our help,
our parents persist in being themselves.
Only from the new lines on their faces,
do I know I'm aging.

Siblings—archives of our earliest incarnations.

וַיִּגַּשׁ

≅

Vayigash

≅

(And he drew near)

" 'The intentions in a person's heart are deep waters, but a person of understanding can draw them out . . . .' So was Joseph deep, and Judah came to draw from him."

—Tanḥuma Yashan

Ars Poetica

In a land and language not his own,
Joseph made the best of what he'd been given:
his royal robes more costume than clothes,
he wore illusion as if it were identity.
Yet within him, a well brimmed
with living waters he could draw from
only in service of others. Exiled
from himself, he was always thirsty.

Standing before this powerful man, this
presumed Egyptian, unaware it was
his brother Joseph, before Judah spoke,
he listened. There were the pronouncements
of Joseph's mouth but also—because
without our knowledge or consent, our bodies
bend toward truth—the more honest
messages of his movements.

Only with such attention could Judah
summon the stone from the mouth
of the well, could he offer a story of their family's
travails in such detail an entire camp rose
to busy the palace floor: decades of cooksmoke
blackening the vaulted ceiling, his brothers
aging to men before his eyes, his father's
hair draining to white over vision
dimmed by grief for the lost son who
now listened transfixed to these images

that twined his spine like a length
of rope, bucketing up all the questions
swimming silently inside him, bringing water
from his eyes, his voice to the surface, so he was able,
finally, to answer this story with his own.

The right words ready as pail, cord, and winch
to draw out even the deepest waters.

"When Jacob's sons returned from Egypt, they asked Serah, daughter
of Asher, known for her wisdom and skill with a harp, to gently relay
the news to their father that his son Joseph was not dead. Upon
hearing it, Jacob blessed her, saying, 'The mouth that told me
Joseph is alive will never taste death.'"

—*Sefer HaYashar*

Another Kind

Her grandfather stood in prayer, extolling, cajoling,
thumping his chest with his fist as though to break

a breach for God. Serah, in his shadow, swayed
as he swayed, her fingers like breeze on her harp strings,

her song just another layer of light. Again and again, she
swayed and breathed, *As the sun, as the wind, your son*

Joseph lives, her voice a fig tree unfurling its leaves, a
prickly pear filling with rain. Serah, the Torah's first poet.

Serah, undying, found in every generation that followed:
who was a slave in Egypt, the first to know Moses

as a true prophet; Serah, who wandered the wilderness
as the cloth that shielded the Tabernacle, סֶרַח הָעֹדֵף *serah ha-odef*

(the overlapping excess), the dayenu promise that though
just enough would have been sufficient, there will always be

a little more; Serah, who entered the Promised Land, overlapping
one age with the next. Her voice tasted death

only in others; Serah, the witness, repository
of her people's stories. And who

is she now? Santa Fe yogi, angel
investor, Provincetown captain, theatre director.

What healer, what bridge,
what shelter, what builder, what writer

as prophet? No husband, no children, her songs
were her progeny. Serah, *selah.* Matriarch of my line.

According to the United Nations High Commissioner for Refugees,
since 2008 an annual average of 21.5 million people have been
displaced by disasters relating to the climate crisis, including conflict,
droughts, and famine.

"And all the lands came to Egypt, to Joseph, to get provisions, for the
famine was strong in all the lands."
                                                      —Genesis 41:57

That We May Live and Not Die:
A Deep-Time Report on Climate Refugees

א. *Vision Statement*

    a. On the riverbank, cows grazed, each strapping as a full moon. Seven more rose from the water, gaunt as new moons, and devoured the healthier herd. Yet even after that cannibal's feast, their flanks hung slack as empty grain sacks.

    b. In a gleaming field of wheat, from a single stalk waved seven shibboleths of golden grain, humming in the sunlight. Behind them rose seven more, wind-beaten and scorched, clattering like the tails of rattlesnakes, and they unbraided their withered grains and swallowed the others down whole.

    c. Pharoah woke with a gasp, spirit clanging like a five-alarm fire.

    d. And even as his limbs were scrubbed and perfumed by the Chief of Scented Oils for Rubbing His Majesty's Body, the dreams insisted:
        i. cows eating cows, wheat eating wheat;
            (a) something was coming.

ב. *Research Methodology*

    a. Because no soothsayer nor lobbyist nor priest could explain, *b.* the chief butler stepped forward. Freshly restored from a prison stint due to Pharoah's disfavor, he spoke of a foreigner who'd shared his cell and had a knack for interpreting dreams.

    c. Like a secret gold-bearing vein,
        i. Joseph was extracted from the darkness of the prison pit.

ג. *Data Analysis*

    a. Guards held the foreign youth between them while Pharoah recounted his dreams.

    b. And though he was struggling to see, still blinking against the sudden sunlight, Joseph spoke from sight divinely inspired: For years to come, food will be so plentiful the poor shall eat mutton at every meal and hogs will be slopped with spiced stews and tiger-nut cakes.
        i. Yet soon enough, he continued, with knowledge beyond his knowing, *famine will unhinge its jaw and no evidence of abundance will remain.*

ד. *In Times of Plenty (Theirs)*

    a. With Joseph's mouth designated God's divining cup,
        i. he became Egypt's righthand man.

    b. Traveling the country, he gathered rations like the shore gathers sand, in quantities beyond counting.
        i. In each silo, along with grain, he placed a pinch of the soil from which it had grown—
            (a) a bit of ancient agrarian magic to keep it all from rotting.

ה. *In Times of Scarcity (Ours)*

    a. Whether from flood or drought or war
        i. the predicted famine arrives.

b. Desperation gives nations legs.

c. Toward the lands of accumulated abundance
    i. come those desperate enough to risk
        (a) crossing deserts clanking with bottles that hold their meager water
            (i) (parents the only source of shade for their children),
        (b) crossing oceans in patchwork boats
            (i) (a child, facedown, washed up on the shore),
        (c) crossing mountain passes in sandals and makeshift shoes, what they owned reduced to what they can carry
            (i) (children lashed like packs to their backs),
                c.i. leaving the creatures and trees they know by leaf and pelt and song,
                c.ii. leaving the land that felt familiar as family, hoping for the mercy of unknown places.
                    (1) Any loss better than the certainty of burying your children.

1. *Operating Costs*

a. In the relentless wind, even the faces of the young are worn to bark,
    i. fissured and disfigured by sandstorms rising from an earth that shares their thirst.

b. Like Joseph's mother Rachel, too many are lost on the journey.
    i. Fever eats those with too little to eat, devouring the last of their water and weight
        (a) until most who die, die in the night,
            (i) the cold more than their bodies can bear.

c. Roads lined with bodies of the dead or nearly so—
    i. those walking past too weary to stop and stoop and see.
        (a) Spirits left to wander that bardo of on-the-way. Origins decimated, destinations unwelcoming.

d. Without a preserving pinch of soil to place in their new homes,

    i. even those who survive, hunger for the place that raised them

        (a) and know the erosion begun by that longing.

e. And so many of those who ma*ke it are made to leave their identities behind.*

    i. Even the skilled, the educated, forced

    (a) to drive cabs,

    (b) clean toilets,

    (c) build pyramids.

ɪ. *Conclusions (Then & Now & Too Many Times Between)*

a. Yet many adapt

    i. so skillfully the children of their children's children forget

    (a) their family ever called another place home.

b. They forget those now arriving follow routes forged by the feet of Joseph's brothers:

    i. Who, starving, left everything they knew behind.

    ii. Who arrived in a new land

    iii. where they found provisions and the promise of plenty,

    iv. so reached back across the border

    v. to bring their families to join them.

        (a) Over their caravan, a banner emblazoned with the words of their father:

            (i) That we may live and not die.

c. They forget, as they barricade the borders their families once crossed,

    i. that the book they claim is central to their lives has at its center:

    (a) "You shall not oppress a stranger,

    (b) for you know the soul of the stranger,

    (c) for you were once strangers in the land of Egypt."

    d. For as soon as Joseph's family began to thrive in their new land,

        i. as soon as they believed themselves indistinguishable from their neighbors,

            (a) they were turned against by those who'd once welcomed them.

ח. *Recommendations*

    a. Remember

        i. these stories are old ones.

            (a) And they repeat.

וַיְחִי

≅

Vayechi

≅

(And he lived)

"And God said to Israel in visions of the night, 'Jacob! Jacob!' and he answered, 'Here I am.' Now God said, 'I am God, the God of your father. Do not be afraid of going down to Egypt, for a great nation will I make of you there. I Myself will do down with you to Egypt, and I Myself will bring you up, yes, up again.'"

—Genesis 46:2-5

And God speaks

in a sound beyond
sounding: A ready well

in the driest desert.
Your mother's palm,

just before sleep,
cupping your small cheek. The still

small voice you've known
all your life. You'd always

assumed it was yours
alone, just like

you'd always assumed
you were alone.

Jacob's Gift

Mid-step, no warning, a healthy person's
spirit would flee their nostrils with a sneeze—
the Talmud says such sudden deaths
were once the only deaths.

        So it wouldn't have been uncommon
                  how my grandmother
      found him: her husband
        slumped at the breakfast table,
            face resting on his crossed arms
      like a student asleep in a library carrel.

But when an aging Jacob reached for life's next rung
and found only air, he prayed for more time.
So God created illness.
    So Jacob lay in what he thought was his deathbed
    and summoned his sons. He promised
revelations, and naming was
its own kind of prophecy. For Jacob
called each man as he was
and as his tribe would be:

    Reuben was unstable water; Simeon and Levi,
    lawless weapons, and on down the line—
    a lion's whelp, ships' haven,
    strong-boned ass, viper by the path, raider
    of raiders, fat loaf of bread, hind let loose,
    wild colts on a hillside, ravenous wolf.

      Twenty years now
      without him and my grandfather's voice
      is still the one I'd most like to hear; his,
      the counsel I've most needed.

Before his final breakfast,
he'd walked three miles, lifted weights.
    I'm sorry, Grandpa, but what would I give
    to have given you Jacob's gift,
    to have watched you weaken
        as I sat by your bed,
        your hand gone frail
    in mine. To have had you call me
    by my right names:

rain-soothed lake, kitchen mandolin, lawyers'
snakelet, students' refuge, cuss-headed mule,
plodder on the path, striver of strivers,
gluten-free toast, curator of commas, association
maker—or insufficient namer, bereft as I am
of all death took when it took you too quickly.

"Just as Joseph was in the lap of [his father] Jacob seventeen years,
Jacob was in the lap of Joseph seventeen years."

—*Rabbi David Kimhi*

Reciprocity

For I was mud and you were the face
pressed to mine, making me in your image.
When I was a furnacing fever, you were a dousing river.
I, word-hunger and you, the book by heart.
I, new blooming; you, pages of my pressed petals.
And when I was ambition, you were the open hand,
guiding, supporting, letting me go.

Now, when you have faltered, I am the hand
that guides, supports, promises
not to let go. Your memories, blossoms
browning on the vine, your tongue hungry
for right words, I am the book of your life, offering you
back to you. You furnace with fear; I am the river
to calm your feet in. And when, one day, you
finally rest, I will be the face
that keeps your face in the world.

"Because you sped toward your anger like water speeds on its course,
you shall no longer receive the abundance that was meant for you."
—Jacob to Reuven, his firstborn son (Rashi on Genesis 49:4)

Like Water on Its Course

א.

Every page, every day, a rigged game: each human a character
pricked by sentience, conscious of the joystick's jerk.

Even before birth, Samson was blessed into service,
his parents given holy notice. God's will conducted

the command center in his head: *There's a lion in the vineyard,*
Samson; tear it asunder. Here's the jawbone of an ass; there,

the faces of your enemies; and here's the arc of the swing.
The more chosen you are, the less free you are

to choose. And by chapter's end: betrayed, shorn, blinded,
and dead by his own God-directed hands—

but a murderer, too. That fact just as true.
Or is a sin compelled somehow less sinful?

ב.

For if not to God, aren't we captive
to our minds' wiring, our bodies' chemistry, the family

we're born to? The anger that is my birthright—
passed down from my father and his father unto him,

corrosive, self-starting—it biles up in me. A surge of fury,
I grow strong with it: my scalp singes and tightens, my muscles

flex and sing. I try to soothe it with reason, to bury it
in my chest, but it burns there like a second heart.

ל.
The lion was the only kill Samson hid
from his parents. Left to rot until bees hived the mighty ribs,

when Samson plunged wrist-deep into the remains,
he emerged with palmfuls of honey—a false balm

that roiled his gut. For whether Samson was gripped
by God or rage, the lion he killed was just as dead.

ז.
Which part is God: my temper or my tempering of it?

I need to believe it's both, that even the worst of me
is somehow holy. That I can channel what I cannot change.

How to Pray

Forget ecstasy, that easy leap outside the body.
Our bodies are already up on blocks, listing
and unsightly in the yard. No. The way to God
is not around the world but through it. So dig
your heels into your heels; flex your fists, your
jaw. Then release to become for an instant all
ear: listen out, listen up to branch sawing branch
like a giant violin; listen in—there's your blood's
steady loop-the-loop. Cue eyes: a seizure of light
through the leaves. And tongue: slick of iron
from a nicked gum and, once again, you're five,
last little tooth on its last little strand, wagging
with your breath like a swing. Now, nose: breathe
in the dirt, astir as it is with beetles and rot and light-
seeking shoots. And, finally, be all skin: like a kid's
face pressed to an aquarium window,
presence up so hard to the edge of your husk
you're joined with the wind rivering the cool air
to silk. Only then should you give yourself to joy, dive
from the twin heights of your eyes. And that tiny pool
below, the one you're hurtling toward? It's not God—
well, not exactly. It's you. One breath deeper than you've
ever been, one breath closer to the heeded, heedful world.

"Everything can be taken . . . but one thing: the last of the human
freedoms—to choose one's attitude in any given set of circumstances,
to choose one's own way"

—Viktor E. Frankl

In the Breath Between

All is foreseen, said Rabbi Akiva,
and freedom is given, holding
in each hand the tail of a horse
straining away from the other.

Abandoned, enslaved, imprisoned,
and exiled—the first horse
was everything Joseph suffered.

Yet when he could have killed
his betraying brothers with a nod
of his head, he forgave them instead,
saying, *It was not you*
who sent me here, but God. His choice
           of mercy was the second horse.

If all that happens
                 is fate, who we are
is the meaning we make from it.
           And in that breath
       between what's done to us
         and what we do with it
is the crucible of our becoming.

"Blessed are you, God our God, Sovereign of the World, who has given us the Torah of truth, planting within us life everlasting."
—*the prayer recited after an* עֲלִיָּה *aliyah (a going up) to read from the Torah*

Aliyah

Let me speak to you as the tree I climbed as a child,
the one in the far corner of my grandmother's yard,
whose bark was a tapestry of rough diamonds.
Your first branch was low enough to leap to,
textured enough to hold me. And each branch after
placed as though to keep me climbing.
I paused only to press my ear to your trunk
and hear it: the heartbeat of water
moving toward the leaves, the conversation
between roots and sky. Climbing until my hair
twined your needles' spines; until, anointed
by your green, you took root within me; so I speak
from the part of me who grows you, grows
with you, who will always live in your branches.
And in the boughs, so many there with me.
A vantage we could not have reached
on our own, a vision otherwise beyond us.
All of us, in that overstory, unalone.

NOTES

In Jewish study, there is a tradition of not just citing your sources but also naming your teachers, as well as the teachers of those teachers, recognizing and raising up the names of those whose wisdom shaped you and reaffirming that God alone creates something from nothing. I have tried to give such acknowledgments here.

The translations found throughout this book are an amalgam of the brilliant translations of Robert Alter, Everett Fox, Avivah Zornberg, the Jewish Publication Society's 1985 translation, and, on occasion, my own far lesser efforts.

The opening epigraph is from Rabbi Lawrence Kushner's *God Was in This Place & I, i Did Not Know: Finding Self, Spirituality and Ultimate Meaning* (Jewish Lights Publishing, 2016) and continues, "We read the Bible, fix our attention on a phrase, and suddenly find ourselves in a conversation with centuries of teachers . . . convinced that holy words are intimately related not only to what God means but even to who God is and who we are." The second epigraph is from Adrienne Rich's *What is Found There: Notebooks on Poetry and Politics* (Norton, 2003).

"Stepping through the Gate"—Among the first advice offered in פִּרְקֵי אָבוֹת *Pirkei Avot* (Ethics of the Fathers), a collection of wisdom teachings included in nearly all traditional Jewish prayer books, is, "Be deliberate in judgement, raise up many students, and make a fence around the Torah" (1:1). This poem was commissioned by the North Carolina Museum of Art, written in response to an 18th century יָד *yad* (a Torah pointer) in their Judaica collection.

בְּרֵאשִׁית ∘ *Bereshit* ∘ (In the Beginnings)
Most often translated as "In the beginning," if read literally the name of this parshah is plural, so has multiple translations including, "In the beginnings."

"In the beginnings"—Of these beginnings, scholar Avivah Zornberg wrote, "The act of *Havdalah*, separation, is central . . . the main business of that day was the radical transformation of reality from the encompassing oneness of God to the possibility of more-than-one . . . [followed by] the yearning of the split-off parts of the cosmos for a primordial condition of unitary being" (*The Beginning of Desire*). Or, as *Genesis Rabbah*, a collection of ancient rabbinic writing on Genesis, puts it, "Why doesn't it say, 'It was good' on the second day? Because on that day divisiveness was created."

The shape of the poem is inspired by Rabbi Isaac Luria's concept of צִמְצוּם *tzimtzum*: the contraction of God's infinite self in order to create a

space, a void, at God's center in which our world and the free will of those within that world could exist—a space that was then shot through with a ray of divine energy, which serves as the activating force within every manifestation of creation.

"And God speaks [words that enter the world]"—In Hebrew, דָּבָר *davar* means both "word" and "thing," reflecting a deep belief in the creative energy of language.

"Prayer should be a tunnel"—This poem is dedicated to Josefa Briant.

"Creation Stories"—In the first two chapters of Genesis, there are two separate stories of the world's creation, as well as of the humans within it.

In the first, God says, "Let us make a human in our image" (Gen 1:26): אָדָם *adam* (a human), is derived from the Hebrew אֲדָמָה *adamah* (earth) and is a generic name for a human being—not definitively male. This allows Genesis 1:27 to make far more sense when it seems to speak of a human with two sexes: "And God created the earthperson in God's image, in the image of God, God created it; male and female God created them" (this is the basis for the story in Plato's *The Symposium* about humans with four arms, four legs, two sets of genitalia, and a single head with two faces, which introduced the idea of "soulmates"). Gratitude to Phyllis Tribble for this translation and Burt Visotzky for introducing me to it.

The second creation story is far more familiar: God as sculptor, surgeon, and matchmaker, molding man from the earth (Adam from *adamah*) and then forming Eve from his rib: " . . . God formed man from the dust of the earth. God blew into his nostrils the breath of life . . . but for Adam no fitting helper was found. So, God cast a deep sleep upon the man; and while he slept, God took one of his ribs . . . [and] fashioned the rib that God had taken from the man into a woman" (Gen 2:7, 2:20-22).

"Imposter Syndrome Among the Thorns and Thistles"—The epigraph is part of the burden placed upon Adam and Eve after their expulsion from Eden. This was first written as an epistolary poem to Matthew Olzmann for inclusion in his poetry collection *Constellation Route* and is dedicated to Matthew.

"Sleepwalkers in the Garden"—After eating from the Tree of Knowledge, Adam and Eve "heard the sound of God moving about in the garden at the breezy time of day; and the man and his wife hid from God among the trees of the garden" (Gen 3:8).

"Free will"—A study by University of Utah's Biology Department found indications that the proportions of the human hand, capable of precision control, a powerful grip, and making a fist buttressed by the thumb, reflect an evolution driven in part by selection for the improved ability to fight. This poem is dedicated to Dr. Jeremy Morris, who introduced me to this study and who continues to further the knowledge of this field.

"At Age 969, Methuselah Gives a Valedictory Address"—Adam's great-grandson ten generations on and the grandfather of Noah, Methuselah was the longest-lived person mentioned in the Torah, said to have lived until age 969, when he died just before the Flood (Gen 5:21-27). This poem is dedicated to David O'Hara, whose question posed to his Augustana theology students gave rise to this poem.

"And the Ground Opens Its Mouth to Speak"—When the world's first children made their sacrifices to God, Abel "brought the choicest of the firstborn of his flock," while Cain merely brought an offering "from the fruit of the soil" (Gen 4:3-4). This is often interpreted as a lack of כַּוָנָה *kavanah* (intention) on Cain's part, an offering by rote. Despite God's assurance that he could improve, Cain instead became the first murderer; Abel, the world's first death. So, God condemns Cain to be a "restless wanderer" for whom the soil will bear no sustenance and marks him so that all who meet Cain will know he is protected by God and must be left to live out his punishment (Gen. 4:11-15).

In her groundbreaking work, *The Hebrew Bible and Environmental Ethics: Humans, NonHumans, and the Living Landscape* (Cambridge University Press, 2019), Mari Joerstad tracks how the authors of the Torah "viewed nonanimal nature as active and alive, that is, as persons . . . able to hear and obey commands, protest human misconduct, lament and offer praise, and affect human history" (3). This poem is dedicated to Mari.

נֹחַ ∘ *Noach* ∘ (Noah/Rest)
"Collective Nouns"—In the Torah, God observes of humanity that "every scheme of his heart was perpetually evil" and, in a verse made especially poignant by how rarely God's internal state is described in the Torah, it is written, "God was sorry to have made humankind on earth and it pained God's heart" (Gen 6:5-7). So, God instructs Noah, the most righteous man of his corrupt generation, to build an ark for himself, his unnamed wife, his sons and their wives, and two members, male and female, of "unclean" animal species, seven pairs of "clean" animals deemed fit for sacrifice, all of which, after the Flood, will be the seeds of earth's second incarnation. Despite the Midrash saying it took Noah 120 years to build the ark, despite 40 days and 40 nights of rain and 150 more days until they anchored on Mount Ararat, Noah is not recorded as having uttered a single word until they reached dry land. "Never tasting the taste of sleep," paraphrases *Midrash Tanhuma, Noah, 7.*

The epigraph is from a 2019 report from the U.N.'s Human Rights Council, written by U.N. poverty and human rights official Philip Alston, which said, "Perversely, the richest, who have the greatest capacity to adapt and are responsible for and have benefitted from the vast majority of greenhouse gas emissions, will be the best placed to cope with climate change, while the poorest, who have contributed the least to emissions and have the least capacity to react, will be the most harmed."

"And God speaks"—The epigraph is from Genesis 8:15-17.

"After the Flood"—Though God acknowledges "the devisings of the human heart are evil from youth," God smells the pleasing fragrance of the burnt offerings offered by Noah's clan after the Flood and promises in "God's heart" that "I will not again strike down all living things as I did" (Gen 8:20-22). The formal reminder of that covenant with humanity is the rainbow: "Behold, I am making a covenant with you and with your offspring after you. And with every living creature that is with you . . . that never again will all flesh be cut off by flood waters, never again will flood waters destroy the earth" (Gen 9:9-11).

"Elegy in Prophetic Perfect"—"The perfect [tense] serves to express actions, events, or states, which the speaker wishes to represent from the point of view of completion, whether they belong to a determinate past time, or extend into the present, or while still future, are pictured as in their completed state," Wilhelm Gensenius wrote in *Gensenius' Hebrew Grammar* (Pantianos Classics, 1812). "This use of the perfect occurs most frequently in prophetic language (perfectum propheticum). The prophet so transports himself in imagination into the future that he describes the future event as if it had been already seen or heard by him."

"In the Shadow of Babel"—When the Tower of Babel was built, "the whole earth was of one language" (Gen 11:1), which the Netziv (Rabbi Naftali Zvi Yehudah Berlin) interpreted to mean Babel was the world's first manifestation of totalitarianism: "And since the opinions of people are not identical, they feared that people might abandon this philosophy and adopt another. . . . And one who veered from this uniformity among them was judged with burning" (*Haamek Davar*, Gen 11:3). This poem is dedicated to my Five Points neighbors whose generous presence made the pandemic bearable: Kelly Gloger and Bonnie Luria, Lauren Biehl and Luce Beagle, Marta Donahoe and Mike Buncher, Duke Ramuten and the Possums of

Possum Splendor. And to Robin Wall Kimmerer, whose *Braiding Sweetgrass: Indigenous Wisdom, Scientific Knowledge, and the Teaching of Plants* (Milkweed Editions, 2015) is an invaluable resource and inspiration.

לֶךְ-לְךָ ◦ *Lech-Lecha* ◦ (Go forth)

"Mazel Tov"—לֶךְ-לְךָ *Lech-lecha* begins the command God gives Abram, later renamed Abraham, to send him on his journey toward becoming the first patriarch of the Jewish people. The plainest translation of this term is "Go forth" but this poem also draws on alternate translations compiled by Rabbi Jonathan Sacks (ל״ז): Go for yourself," which Rashi interpreted to mean you must believe in what you can become; "Go with yourself," carry with you your beliefs and way of life; "Go by yourself," have the courage to take an often lonely journey; and the mystical "Go to yourself," which R. David of Lelov characterized as the journey to the root of the soul.

"Sing, O Barren One, Who Did Not Bear a Child"—God commands Abram to leave his family and the place of his birth to find a promised land so that God may make of him "a great nation" (Gen 12:2). Sarah, the first of the Torah's matriarchs and the first wife of Abram, is introduced as Sarai. When Abram is 86 and has no children, Sarai suggests he sleep with her handmaid Hagar, who then gives birth to Ishmael. When seven years later Sarai has still not had a child, God appears to Abram in a dream and promises again that he would be the scion of a great nation. As Rashi wrote, "[God] said to him . . . Abram has no son but Abraham will have a son. Likewise, Sarai will not give birth, but Sarah will give birth. I shall call you [by] another name and [your] destiny will be changed" (Rashi on Gen. 15:5). Elsewhere, Sarah is identified as "Iscah," the daughter of Abraham's brother, and her status as a prophet was partially derived from a possible etymology of this name (*Babylonian Talmud*: Megillah, 14a:13).

"How the Angel Found Her"—Though Sarai offers Abram her handmaid Hagar to have a child on her behalf, once Hagar is pregnant, Sarai is displeased and treats Hagar so harshly she flees into the wilderness. There, she is met by an angel who urges her to return to the home of Sarai despite the awful treatment, assuring Hagar of countless offspring in a promise very similar to the one made to Abraham and furthermore saying the child she carries shall be named יִשְׁמָעֵאל *Ishmael* (God will hear) (Gen 16:1-11).

"Covenant Between the Pieces"—In this second covenant between God and Abraham, known as the "Abrahamic Covenant," God reveals to Abraham that though his descendants will be strangers in a strange land, oppressed and enslaved for many generations, God would ultimately redeem them, and they would inherit their holy land. This covenant was sealed with the "Covenant of the Pieces." For this, Abraham rendered a prescribed set of animals in halves and then fell into a deep sleep in which he witnessed the appearance of a smoking oven and watched a flaming torch pass between the pieces. These, Rashi wrote, were "representative of the Divine Shechinah which is spoken of as fire" (Gen 15:1-21). The שְׁכִינָה *Shekhinah* (a dwelling place for, or a manifestation of God's presence) is often understood to represent the feminine attributes of the divine. In *Eikkah Rabbah*, an idol is called a צָרָה *tzarah* (rival wife). The epigraph is from Audre Lorde's essay "The Uses of Anger: Women Responding to Racism" (*Sister Outsider: Essays & Speeches,* Crossing Press, 1984).

וַיֵּרָא ° *Vayera* ° (And he appeared)
"Will not the Judge of the Earth do justice?"—When the angels urge Lot, nephew of Abraham, to take his unnamed wife and their two unmarried daughters out of Sodom before God destroys it, leaving his two married daughters behind with their husbands, one angel says, "Flee for your life! Do not look behind you, nor stop anywhere in the Plain; flee to the hills, lest you be swept away." But Lot's wife looks back and is turned into a pillar of salt (Gen 19:17-26). The Midrash on this is plentiful and contradictory, much of it an attempt to justify this harsh fate. According to Rashi, she denied salt to visiting angels, while *Genesis Rabbah* told a story in which she went to a neighbor's on the pretext of borrowing salt, but it was really to gossip about her visitors, which brought the wrath of the townspeople to her door (19:26:2) and, as Rashi wrote, "by salt she sinned and by salt she was punished." Yet in *Sefer HaYashar, The Book of the Righteous*, she is moved to look back by compassion for the two daughters she was forced to leave behind and becomes an eternally regenerating salt pillar, providing essential

nutrients to the cattle of that place to this day. This poem is dedicated to my sister Nicole Filip and her sons, my nephews, Matthew and Jacob.

"Learning to Run Barefoot in a Dry Riverbed at Dawn"—This poem is dedicated to Christopher Arbor.

"And God Speaks [How it finds you: at attention:]"—This summons from God begins the עֲקֵדָה *Akedah*, the Binding of Isaac, in which God tests Abraham by commanding he sacrifice his beloved son Isaac on Mount Moriah.

"Why There is No Hebrew Word for *Obey*"— In the Akedah, only once Isaac is bound upon the altar and Abraham has the knife raised above him, does an angel stay his hand and tell him to sacrifice a ram instead. Quoting *Genesis Rabbah*, Rashi wrote that not only was Abraham willing to sacrifice Isaac but even once the ram was substituted he wanted God to know of his willingness to carry out God's will and at "every sacrificial act he performed on [the ram] he prayed, saying, 'May it be Thy will that this act may be regarded as having been done to my son—as though my son is being slain; as though his blood is being sprinkled; as though his skin were being flayed; as though he is being burnt and is being reduced to ashes" (Rashi on Genesis, 22:13). The epigraph is from Eric Hoffer's *Reflections on the Human Condition* (Hopewell Publications, 2006). This poem is dedicated to the eleven congregants killed at the Tree of Life synagogue on October 27, 2018: Joyce Fienberg, Richard Gottfried, Rose Mallinger, Jerry Rabinowitz, Cecil and David Rosenthal, Bernice and Sylvan Simon, Daniel Stein, Melvin Wax, and Irving Younger. May their memories be a blessing.

"Kaddish for the Living"—Though Sarah dies sometime after the Akedah, it's unclear exactly how much time passes between Abraham and Isaac's return from Mount Moriah and the date of her death. Rashi cites *Genesis Rabbah* 58:5, writing that when Sarah learned Isaac "was almost slaughtered, her soul flew out of her body and she died" (Gen 23:2). In Midrash from *Pirkei Rabbi Eliezer*, Satan, upset that Isaac is still alive, goes to Sarah and describes his imagined sacrifice in such great detail she cries out three times then dies.

חַיֵּי שָׂרָה ∘ *Chayei Sarah* ∘ (Life of Sarah)

"From the Cave, Her Voice" and **"And Abraham came to eulogize Sarah and to weep for her."**—Despite being called "Life of Sarah," this parshah deals with events after Sarah's death: her burial by Abraham, Abraham dispatching his servant Eliezer to find a wife for their son Isaac, Abraham granting Isaac his inheritance, and Abraham's death. Sarah is buried in what is known as the Cave of Machpelach, the "double cave," as pairs of matriarchs and patriarchs are said to be buried there: Sarah and Abraham, Rebecca and Isaac, Leah and Jacob. According to some mystical teachings, it's also the entrance to Eden, where Adam and Eve are said to be buried.

"Lemme tell you the one that killed at canasta!"—Three angels appear to Abraham in the guise of three visiting men. When he invites them into his tents for food and drink, they tell him his wife Sarah will have a baby within the year. Overhearing them, 90-year-old Sarah "who has ceased the ways of women" (Gen 18:11), i.e. she is no longer menstruating, laughs—not even out loud but within herself or, depending on the translation, deep within her entrails. Still, God confronts the couple, "Why did Sarah laugh, saying, 'Shall I in truth bear a child, old as I am?' Is anything too wondrous for God?" (Gen 18:13-14). In her fear, Sarah denies her laughter. This poem is dedicated to my grandmother Bernice Jacobs.

"P.O.T.S. Prayer"—Isaac first meets Rebecca when he is meditating in a field (Gen 24:63), which is said to be the basis for the daily מִנְחָה *Mincha* (afternoon prayer). Rabbi Jonathan Sacks wrote, "When the Talmud says, in the context of Isaac, אֵין שִׂיחָה אֶלָּא תְּפִלָּה *ein sichah ela tefillah*, we could translate this phrase as 'conversation is a form of prayer' . . . Thus there are three modes of spirituality, and we experience each in the course of a single day. There is the human quest (Abraham, morning prayer), the divine encounter (Jacob, evening prayer), and the dialogue (Isaac, afternoon)" (*Chayei Sarah*, 5768: Isaac and Prayer). שְׁכִינָה *Shekhinah* is the divine feminine divine, the presence of God that dwells in the world.

"Saturday Services at the Provincetown Shore"—Robert Alter notes, "Holding the genitals, or placing a hand on the genitals, during the act of solemn oath taking is attested in several ancient societies (a fact already noted by Abraham ibn Ezra in the twelfth century)." A מְחִצָּה *mechitza* is a partition used to separate men and women, most often found in Orthodox synagogues and religious celebrations.

"Ordinary Immanence"—Mincha, the traditional Jewish afternoon prayer, is meant to be recited as a pause within the busyness of the day.

"At First Sight, Many Seeings Later"—As it is written in Genesis 24:63-65, "And Isaac went out to stroll in the field toward evening, and he raised his eyes and, look, camels were coming. And Rebecca raised her eyes and saw Isaac, and she תִּפֹּל (*tephal*, a tense of נָפַל *naphal*) from the camel." While יָרַד *yarad* is a word more commonly associated with dismounting from an animal, *naphal* is found throughout the Torah to mean *fall*: as in to fall in battle or fall asleep or even have your face fall in distress but is used most frequently when describing people falling in awe before God. Rebecca and Isaac are the only monogamous couple found among the Biblical foreparents. The epigraph is from the title poem of Jean Valentine's *The River at Wolf* (Alice James Books, 1992) and the seed of this poem was planted by Alicia Jo Rabins' "I Fell Off My Camel," from her album of Midrashic songs "Girls in Trouble" (JDub Records, 2009).

תּוֹלְדֹת ∘ *Toldot* ∘ (Begettings)

"The Bravest of the Birds"—The younger sibling being served by or favored over the elder is a theme throughout Genesis: Abel's sacrifice is accepted while Cain's is not, Isaac is favored over Ishmael and seen to carry on Abraham's lineage, then Jacob receives Isaac's blessing instead of Esau, goes on to love Rachel above her elder sister Leah, and favors their son Joseph above his ten preceding sons and daughter Dinah. This poem is dedicated to my sister Jill Jacobs.

"In the village of my body, two people"—After a long period in which Rebecca is unable to bear children, Isaac prays on her behalf and she becomes pregnant "but the children almost crushed one another inside her, so she said, 'If this be so, why do I exist?'" to which God answers, referring to the twin boys she is carrying, "Two nations are in your body, two peoples from your loins shall issue. One nation shall prevail over the other nation, the elder shall be servant to younger!" (Gen 25:22-23). Esau, the elder, is said to have emerged covered in a mantle of red hair and became a vigorous man of the field. Jacob, the younger, emerged grasping Esau's heel ("Heel-Holder" is one of the translations of his name), and grows up be a "a plain man, staying among the tents" (Gen 25:25-27). This poem is dedicated to Mellie Logan.

"Comfort Food"—The *Babylonian Talmud* states, "On that day Abraham our forefather passed away, Jacob our forefather prepared a lentil stew to comfort Isaac, his father, as it was customary to serve mourners lentil stew. . . . Just as this lentil has no mouth, i.e., it does not have a crack like other legumes, so too a mourner has no mouth, that is, his anguish prevents him from speaking. Alternatively, just as this lentil is completely round, so too mourning comes around to the inhabitants of the world" (*Bava Batra*, 16b:11-12, trans. William Davidson). For gifting me the language to describe the true nature of a hum, gratitude to Rose McLarney.

"Joint Account"—While camped in Gerar, Isaac and his servants redig the wells originally dug by Abraham, which the Philistines had filled in with dirt after Abraham's death. The herdsmen of Gerar dispute his right to these wells, so Isaac calls the first עֵשֶׂק *Esek* (contention) and the second שִׂטְנָה *Sitnah* (harassment). Only once he digs a new well is it left uncontended. He calls this well רְחֹבוֹת *Rehoboth* (ample space), for "Now at last God has granted us ample space to increase in the land" (Gen 26:18-22).

וַיֵּצֵא ◦ *Vayetze* ◦ (And he left)
"And I, i did not know it"—At his mother Rebecca's urging, Jacob impersonates his older brother Esau to receive their father Isaac's blessing for the firstborn. Devastated and enraged by this deception, Esau vows to kill Jacob, who flees to avoid his wrath. Along the way, Jacob makes camp in a particular place where, Rashi notes, "The sun set for him suddenly,

earlier than usual, so that he would indeed spend the night there" (Gen 28:11). And there he has the first of his two evening encounters with God, Who promises both protection and the prodigious continuation of Jacob's lineage: "And he dreamt: here, a ladder was set up on the earth, its top reaching the heavens, and here: messengers of God were going up and down on it" (Gen 28:12). This poem owes a debt to Lawrence Kushner's brilliant exploration of this story in *God Was in This Place & I, i Did Not Know.* The epigraph is from Wendell Berry's poem "To Know the Dark" (*Selected Poems of Wendell Berry*, Counterpoint, 1999).

"Prayers from a Dark Room"—There's little consensus within Judaism on what happens after we die. Some believe the righteous go to הָעוֹלָם הַבָּא *Ha'Olam Ha'Ba* (The World to Come), which many believe is the Garden of Eden. For the rest of us, one possible destination is Gehenna. While some view this is a punishment, close to the Christian version of Hell, others believe it a temporary, neutral place from which to reflect on your life and repent for past misdeeds. "According to the Midrash," wrote Allen Afterman in *Kabbalah and Consciousness* (Sheep Meadow Press, 1992), "the original skin of Adam and Eve was white light (*chasmal*) . . . After the primordial sin, God clothed Adam and Eve with 'skin clothing.' . . . coarse 'skins' somewhat analogous to scar tissue . . . " This poem was commissioned by the Boutelle-Day Poetry Center at Smith College, written in response to Lesley Dill's photograph "Throat: 'I am afraid to own a body, I am afraid to own a soul," a phrase taken from Emily Dickinson's poem "I am afraid to own a Body."

"Another Calling"—In the brief story of Jacob's dream, the word מָקוֹם *makom* (place) occurs six times. As Robert Alter wrote, "This is the tale of the transformation of an anonymous place through vision into Bethel, a 'house of God.'" Yet it also points to one of the traditional names for God: "Why is God called *Makom*? Because God is the place of the world and the world is not God's place" (*Yalqut Shimoni*, Vayetze Remez, 117). In Jacob's waking cry of, "How נוֹרָא *norah* is this place!" *Norah* is from the root יָרֵא *yareh*, a verb often used to describe people's reactions to God, variously translated "to fear," "to stand in awe," and "to feel reverence."

"So Jacob served seven years for Rachel and they seemed to him but a few days because of his love for her."—Robert Alter notes the same pun of וַיַּשְׁקְ *wayashq* (watered/drank) and וַיִּשַׁק *wayishaq* (kissed) is used in the Song of Songs 8:2-3. After the speaker wishes they could kiss the subject of their song, they say they "would let you drink of the spiced wine, of my pomegranate juice."

"Personal Injury Parents"— When Jacob first meets his great love Rachel, daughter of his uncle Laban, "Jacob kissed Rachel, and broke into tears" (Gen 29:11). Avivah Zornberg wrote of this verse, "Jacob desires eternal union with Rachel, and in the very moment when desire is born, he knows that he will be separated from her, by death and burial. It is a strange passion that brings Jacob to tears. Who would think of the grave at the moment of live encounter?" (*The Beginning of Desire*) and Rashi explained it, "For he saw by the Holy Spirit that she would not enter with him for burial." The misremembered line is from Theodore Roethke's "The Waking:" "I learn by going where I have to go" (*Collected Poems of Theodore Roethke*, Doubleday, 1953). This poem is dedicated to Dana Roeser, the original misrememberer of Roethke's verse and a source of wisdom on confronting fear.

"Measure for Measure"—Though Jacob served his uncle Laban seven years to earn the hand of his younger daughter Rachel, on what was to be their wedding night Laban substituted his elder daughter Leah in the darkened nuptial tent. When confronted, Laban said, "It is not the practice in our place to marry off the younger before the older. Wait until the bridal week of this one is over and we will give you that one [meaning Rachel] too, provided you serve me another seven years" (Gen 29:26-27). In *Midrash Rabbah*, "When Jacob confronts Leah for her betrayal she says, 'Is there a master without students? Did your father not call you Esau and you answered him?!'"

"Judaism has long meditated on the concept of עַיִן תַּחַת עַיִן *ayin takhat ayin*—an eye for an eye (Leviticus 24:20)," wrote scholar Ellen Frankel, "interpreting 'eye' not literally but symbolically, to represent monetary compensation due an injured party. This concept of equivalence extends into the metaphysical realm as well, in the principle of [מִדָּה כְּנֶגֶד מִדָּה *midah keneged midah* (measure for measure)]. That is, a person's deeds bear fruit in his or her life, an evil deed sowing disaster, a good deed reward" (*The Five Books of Miriam*).

וַיִּשְׁלַח ∘ *Vayishlach* ∘ (And he sent)
"The Hendiadys of Marriage"—Hendiadys, a Latinized form of a Greek phrase that means "one by means of two," is when two distinct words are bound by an "and" to create a striking image, like "waste and void," "fire and brimstone," "milk and honey."

"No one's loves, no one's wives"—Though some Midrash say they were the youngest daughters of Laban, thus sisters to Leah and Rachel, in the Torah's text Bilhah and Zilpah are identified only as the handmaids of Leah and Rachel, "given" to their husband Jacob as lesser wives or concubines. Yet despite the fact they bore four of the future leaders of Israel's twelve tribes, even in progressive modern prayer books, when the Matriarchs are invoked along with the Patriarchs at the start of the Amidah, only very rarely are Bilhah and Zilpah included. This poem is dedicated to Alicia Ostriker, whose pathbreaking work made this book possible and whose workshop inspired this poem.

"How Many More"—Rashi, citing *Genesis Rabbah* 84:21, wrote, "R Judah said: a twin-sister was born with each of Jacob's sons and they each took a step-sister to wife. (It was these daughters who comforted Jacob)" (Gen 37:35).

"Godwrestling"—Fleeing his uncle's home, on the way to an encounter with his brother Esau whom he has not seen for twenty years, Jacob divides his wives, children, servants, and flocks into two camps, commands his servants to offer Esau a tribute of over 500 heads of livestock, and sends them all across the Jabbok River. That night, on the other side of the river, an unidentified "man wrestled with him until the break of dawn . . . And he said, 'Let me go, for dawn is breaking.' And [Jacob] said, 'I will not let you go unless you bless me.' And he said, 'What is your name?' And he said,

'Jacob.' And he said, 'Not Jacob shall your name from now be said, but Israel, for you have struggled with God and men and won out'" (Gen 32:25-30). One of the translations of יִשְׂרָאֵל *Israel* is "to wrestle with God."

Conjectures about the identity of the man span from angel to demon. Robert Alter wrote, "Appearing to Jacob in the dark of the night, before the morning when Esau will be reconciled with Jacob, he is the embodiment of portentous antagonism in Jacob's dark night of the soul. He is obviously in some sense a doubling of Esau as adversary, but he is also a doubling of all with whom Jacob has had to contend, and he may equally well be an externalization of all that Jacob has to wrestle with within himself" (*The Hebrew Bible: The Five Books of Moses*).

"And Her Name Meant Everything from Judgment and Strife to Vindication"—When Jacob's family moves to the city of Shechem, his daughter Dinah goes to visit with the local women and is seen by the son of that region's ruler. He rapes her and afterward proclaims his love and his desire to marry her. Though Jacob remains silent at this news, his sons—her brothers—are distraught and through an elaborate ruse that entails every man in the city voluntarily getting circumcised, come upon them while still in pain from that procedure and murder them all, rescuing Dinah from the home of her rapist (Gen 34).

Deuteronomy 22 has a series of elaborate rulings about, among other things, sex outside of marriage and acts of sexual violence, including verses 23 and 24, which state if a man comes upon a virgin who is engaged to another man within a town "and lies with her, you shall take the two of them out to the gate of that town and stone them to death: the girl because she did not cry for help in the town, and the man because he violated another man's wife"—she is at fault because the text assumes she somehow could have prevented the rape, while he deserves execution because he violated "another man's wife," not because he violated the woman herself.

וַיֵּשֶׁב ◦ *Vayeshev* ◦ (And he settled)
"Torn Mind"—In Jewish dietary laws, "kosher" refers to foods deemed "fit" for consumption. Among "unfit" food is any animal found dead: "He shall not eat a carcass or anything that was טְרֵפָה *treifah* (torn), thereby

becoming unclean through it" (Leviticus 22:8). Treifah is more familiar in its Yiddish version, *treif*, which has come to mean not just torn but anything judged unkosher, unfit.

"Dream in Which I Give You My Memories as Dreams"—As a boy, Joseph has two dreams of glory, both of which he relates to his brothers. In the first, they are in a field binding sheaves of wheat when each of the eleven brothers' sheaves bow down to Joseph's. In the second, the sun and moon, presumably his father and dead mother, and eleven stars bow to him. Though Joseph is punished for sharing these dreams, the triumph they predict eventually comes to pass. This poem is dedicated to my goddaughter Frances Tehmina Shroff.

"When He Was Not"—When Jacob sends Joseph, the favorite of his twelve sons, out to the field to check up on his brothers' work and report back, they are enraged and throw Joseph in a pit, intending at first to kill him, then deciding to sell him into slavery instead. To cover their treachery, they take the special coat their father had given Joseph, slaughter a goat, and dip the coat in its blood. When they show it to Jacob, he believes it evidence that his son was devoured by a wild beast.

"Wake, you sleepers from your sleep!"—Maimonides wrote in הִלְכוֹת תְּשׁוּבָה *Hilchot Teshuvah*, the *Laws of Repentance*, that "despite the fact that the blowing of the shofar is an explicit decree in the Scripture, it is also an allusion, as if to say: Awake, O you sleepers, awake from your sleep! . . . Search your deeds and turn to God in repentance."

Rabbi Chanina ben Dosa said about the ram on Mt. Moriah, where Abraham went to sacrifice Isaac, "From that ram, which was created at the twilight, nothing came forth which was useless. The ashes of the ram were the base which was upon the top of the inner altar. The sinews of the ram were the strings of the harp whereon David played. The ram's skin was the girdle (around) the loins of Elijah, . . . The horn of the ram of the left side (was the one) wherein He blew upon Mount Sinai. (The horn) of the right side, which is larger than that of the left, is destined in the future to be sounded in the world that is to come" (*Pirkei Rabbi Eliezer*, 31).

מִקֵּץ ∘*Miketz* ∘ (At the end of)

"And who are you supposed to be?"—For Joseph, who was said to place much importance on his appearance, clothes play a significant role in the key moments of his life. His famous coat is a sign of his father's favoritism and also what Joseph's brothers strip from him and dip in blood to make it seem like he was killed by an animal instead of sold into slavery in Egypt, where he ended up as head slave to the Egyptian Potiphar. Potiphar's wife, after trying unsuccessfully to seduce him, then uses one of the garments Joseph leaves when fleeing her bed to falsely accuse him of attempted rape. Finally, the royal clothes he wears after having risen to the position of viceroy help conceal his identity from his brothers when they come to Egypt during a famine.

Alicia Ostriker wrote of Joseph's coat, "It is the dream-garment . . . Like all such signs it faces two ways. A sign of loss—parallel to the garments God makes for Adam and Eve, or the covering with which his two cautious sons cover the drunken Noah, or the hairy glove Jacob wears to defraud his father—yet at the same time a sign of love and a sign of luxury . . ." (*The Nakedness of the Fathers*).

"How Long Before"—Living in Egypt, estranged from his family for years, "Joseph named his firstborn Menasseh/He-Who-Makes-Forget, meaning: God has made-me-forget all my hardships, all my father's house" (Gen 41:54).

"Sibling Beit Midrash"—When a famine falls across all the lands, ten of Joseph's brothers come to Egypt to find food. After more than twenty years of exile in Egypt, Joseph has risen to become the Viceroy of Egypt. When his brothers come to him, requesting supplies, he recognizes them immediately. Yet cowering before this powerful man they presume to be an Egyptian, they cannot see that he was once the seventeen-year-old brother they once abhorred. A בֵּית הַמִּדְרָשׁ *beit ha'midrash* is a hall dedicated to Torah study, often translated as "study hall," and can also refer to a religious school.

וַיִּגַּשׁ ∘ *Vayigash* ∘ (And he drew near)

"Ars Poetica"—Joseph gives his brothers a series of tests, "not only for his sake . . . ," wrote Stephen Mitchell in *Joseph and the Way of Forgiveness*

(St. Martin's Essentials, 2019), "for theirs as well. It would give them the opportunity to reveal themselves to themselves as well as to him." These culminate in Joseph threatening to have Benjamin, his only full brother and the most beloved remaining son of his father, taken into slavery. Judah draws near to Joseph, whom he still knows only as the Egyptian Viceroy who holds the fate of his family in his hands, and offers himself in Benjamin's stead. He then offers one of the longest speeches in the Torah and, "speaking with all the force of his private experience," wrote Avivah Zornberg, "Judah evokes the lost wholeness of the family, and stirs Joseph to his own attempt at self-description." The epigraph is from *Tanhuma Yashan*, as cited by Zornberg: "'The intentions in a person's heart are deep waters, but a person of understanding can draw them out' [Proverbs 20:5] . . . .What does this resemble? A deep pit into which no one could climb down. Then a clever person came and brought a long rope that reached down to the water so he could draw from it. So was Joseph deep, and Judah came to draw from him."

"Another Kind"—In addition to her grandfather Jacob's blessing that death shall have no power over her, the Midrash extolling Serah's long life is based on the facts she is counted both among those who went to Egypt and those who eventually entered the Promised Land, amounting to a lifespan of hundreds of years. This poem drew on the scholarship of Tamar Kadari in the Jewish Women's Archive.

"That We May Live and Not Die: A Deep-Time Report on Climate Refugees"— Pharoah wakes remembering two nightmares in which seven fat cows are devoured by seven lean cows and then seven robust ears of grain are devoured by seven withered ears. Only after his court magicians fail to adequately interpret his dream does he call for Joseph who interprets them as foretelling seven years of plenty followed by seven years of famine. This eventual famine leads to the migration of Joseph's family to Egypt, where they are initially welcomed. But after several prosperous generations there, in which the Israelites thrive and multiply, Pharoah becomes threatened by their increasing numbers and enslaves them, ordering Hebrew midwives to kill all male Israelite babies at birth.

The United Nations High Commissioner for Refugees has found that since 2008, an annual average of 21.5 million people have been forcibly displaced by weather-related sudden onset hazards – such as floods, storms, wildfires, and extreme temperatures . . . "No region is immune from climate change, but the risks of displacement are greatest for countries with high exposure to hazards and with large populations in areas that lack the capacity or resources to adequately prepare" (UNCHR, "FAQs on Climate Change and Disaster Displacement," 2016).

וַיְחִי ∘ *Vayechi* ∘ (And he lived)

"Jacob's Gift"—*Midrash Rabbah* states, "Jacob requested illness, saying to God: 'A man who dies without previous illness does not settle his affairs with his children; but if he were two or three days ill, he would settle his affairs with his children.' Said God to him: 'By your life, you have asked well, and it will commence with you.' Thus it is written: 'It was said to Joseph: Behold, your father is ill.'" This poem is dedicated to the blessed memories of my grandparents Bill & Gloria Goodman.

"Reciprocity"—Joseph lives in his father Jacob's house in Canaan for seventeen years before his brothers betray him and he is sold into slavery in Egypt. More than two decades later, with famine across the land, Jacob comes to Egypt to be with Joseph and, before his death, lives with him there for seventeen years. This poem borrows its form from the prayer "Ki Anu Amecha," which begins, "We are Your people and You are our God"— specifically the version created by the poet Elliot batTzedek, introduced to me by Joy Ladin. This poem is dedicated to my mother Lauren Goodman.

"Like Water on Its Course"—On his deathbed, Jacob names the character of each of his sons, with a number of them called out for their anger. From Dan, whom Jacob calls "a serpent by the path" (Gen 49:9), comes the lineage of Samson.

"How to Pray"—The epigraph is from Stephen Mitchell's *Joseph and the Way of Forgiveness.*

"In the Breath Between"—Rabbi Jonathan Sacks wrote, "Humanity changed the day Joseph forgave his brothers (Gen 50:15-21). When we forgive and are worthy of being forgiven, we are no longer prisoners of our past . . . .For this was the first recorded act of forgiveness in literature." The epigraph is from Frankl's *Man's Search for Meaning* (Beacon Press, 2006).

"Aliyah"—Of the Torah it is written, "She is a tree of life to those who grasp her, and whoever holds to her is happy" (Proverb 3:18).

SELECT BIBLIOGRAPHY

Alter, Robert. *The Hebrew Bible: A Translation with Commentary*. New York, W.W. Norton & Co., 2019.

Fox, Everett. *The Schocken Bible: Volume I, The Five Books of Moses*. New York, Schocken Books, 1995.

Frankel, Ellen. *Five Books of Miriam: A Woman's Commentary on the Torah*. New York: Harper Collins, 1998.

Graves, Robert, and Raphael Patai, *Hebrew Myths: The Book of Genesis*, New York: Greenwich House, 1983.

Isaiah, Abraham Ben, and Benjamin Sharfman. *The Pentateuch and Rashi's Commentary: Genesis*. Brooklyn, S. S. & R. Publishing Company, Inc., 1976.

Ostriker, Alicia Suskin. *The Nakedness of the Fathers: Biblical Visions & Revisions*. New Jersey: Rutgers University Press, 1994.

Sacks, Jonathan. Divrei Torah on *Genesis* found in "Covenant & Conversation," *rabbisacks.org*.

Visotzky, Burton L. *The Genesis of Ethics: How the Tormented Family of Genesis Leads Us to Moral Development*. New York, Three Rivers Press, 1996.

————. *Reading the Book: Making the Bible a Timeless Text*. Philadelphia, The Jewish Publication Society, 2005.

Zornberg, Avivah Gottlieb. *The Beginning of Desire: Reflections on Genesis*. New York, Image Books, 1996.

ACKNOWLEDGMENTS

My thanks to the editors and staff of the publications in which these poems first appeared, often in different forms and with different titles, for shepherding these words into the world and often improving them with their insights.

32 Poems, "Ordinary Immanence"

About Place, "At Age 969, Methuselah Gives His Valedictory Address"

America, "P.O.T.S. Prayer"

Anacapa Review, "Perseverance Prayer" and "Ars Poetica"

Barrow Street, "How the Angel Found Her"

Bellingham Review, "So Jacob served seven years for Rachel and they seemed to him but a few days because of his love for her" and "Comfort Food"

Bennington Review, "And Abraham came to eulogize Sarah and to weep for her."

Brain Mill Press, "Before the Beginning"

Copper Nickel, "In the village of my body, two people"

EcoTheo Review, "Torn Mind" and "And Her Name Meant Everything from Judgment and Strife to Vindication"

Ecotone, "Collective Nouns"

Four Way Review, "Sing, O Barren One, Who Did Not Bear a Child"

Image, "Godwrestling" and "That We May Live and Not Die"

Jewish Boston, "Lemme tell you the one that killed at canasta" and "After the Flood"

Journal of Feminist Studies in Religion, "No one's loves, no one's wives" and "Wake, you sleepers from your sleep!"

Kosmos Quarterly, "Joseph recognized his brothers, but they did not recognize him" and "Jacob's Gift"

Laurel Review, "Another Calling" and "And who are you supposed to be?"

Lavender Review, "Joseph recognized his brothers, but they did not recognize him"

The Massachusetts Review, "Creation Stories"

Mississippi Review, "In the Beginning" and "And I, i Did Not Know It"

Moment, "Aliyah"

NELLE, "The Question I've Wanted to Hide" and "And the Ground Opens its Mouth to Speak"

New England Review, "Prayer Should be a Tunnel"

On the Seawall, "Prayers from a Dark Room"

Orion, "Learning to Run Barefoot in the Riverbed at Dawn"

Parabola, "How to Pray" and "Sleepwalkers in the Garden"

Pedestal Magazine, "Reciprocity"

Ploughshares, "Free Will" and "Measure for Measure"

Poetry Northwest, "Saturday Services at the Provincetown Shore"

Salamander, "Dream in which I Give You My Memories as Dreams"

Southern Cultures, "Make a fence" and "Mazel Tov"

Southern Humanities Review, "Elegy in Prophetic Perfect," "Why There is No Hebrew Word for Obey," and "Joint Account"

The Southern Review, "Should Not the Judge of the World Do Justice?" and "When He Was Not"

Still: The Journal, "Personal Injury Parents" and "The Hendiadys of Marriage"

Talking River, "Imposter Syndrome Among the Thorns and Thistles"

VIDA Review, "At First Sight, Many Seeings Later" and "The Bravest of the Birds"

West Branch, "Covenant Between the Pieces," "Another Kind," and "How Many More"

Anthologies & Broadsides

Between Paradise and Earth: Eve Poems (Orison Press), "Creation Stories" and "Sleepwalkers in the Garden"

Elemental: Earth (Center for Humans and Nature Press), "And the Ground Opens Its Mouth to Speak"

The Global South (Indiana University Press), "In the Beginning"

In the Tempered Dark: Contemporary Poems Transcending Elegy (Black Lawrence Press), "Sing, O Barren One, Who Did Not Bear a Child," "Kaddish for the Living," and "How Long Before"

The Map of Every Lilac Leaf: Poets Respond to the Smith College Museum of Art (Smith College Museum of Art), "Prayers from a Dark Room"

Poetry in Plain Sight: Broadsides (North Carolina Poetry Society),
  "Sleepwalkers in the Garden"
The Power of the Feminine "I" (Thresh Press), "Creation Stories"
RUMORS SECRETS & LIES: Poems about pregnancy, abortion, & choice
  (Anhinga Press), "Sing, O Barren One, Who Did Not Bear a Child"
What Things Cost: an anthology for the people (University Press of
  Kentucky), "In the Shadow of Babel"
You Are the River (North Carolina Museum of Art), "Make a fence"
Matthew Olzmann's *Constellation Route* (Alice James Books), "Imposter
  Syndrome Among the Thorns and Thistles"

Reprints
Artemis Journal, "And the Ground Opens its Mouth to Speak"
Brain Mill Press, "Covenant Between the Pieces"
Guesthouse Lit, "Relish: An Internet Archive:" "Creation Stories"
Kolture, "Aliyah"
Pensive, "Imposter Syndrome Among the Thorns and Thistles" and
  "Sleepwalkers in the Garden"
Plant-Human Quarterly, "Stepping through the Gate"
Plume, "Imposter Syndrome Among the Thorns and Thistles"
Poetry International: Poems of the Spirit, "Prayer should be a tunnel"
Ritualwell, "Prayer Should be a Tunnel", "Mazel Tov," and "Prayers from a
  Dark Room"
Under a Warm Green Linden, "In the Shadow of Babel"
Witness: Appalachia to Hatteras, "How to Pray," "Mazel Tov," and "Sing,
  O Barren One, Who Did Not Bear a Child"

∞

Burt Visotzky often tells his students, "To study and teach Torah means I
must live Torah, which means I will be present and available to you." For
me, Burt has been not only present and available but, with unflagging
enthusiasm and joy, has become a beloved friend and teacher who
welcomed me past the fences that would have kept me from the research
and writing of this book, while offering a model of what it means to live
what we learn and share.

Nickole Brown asked the questions needed to open these poems and let them breathe. Laure-Anne Bosselaar offered the shelter of her jacaranda and constant friendship. Harry Jacobs, my father, teaches me daily about endurance, bravery, and love. Nicole Filip, my sister, is always there, ready to make me laugh in even the most difficult moments. Even if she can no longer read them, my mother, Lauren Goodman, is a part of every poem I write.

Rose McLarney's questions and suggestions sharpened and strengthened nearly every one of these poems. Exchanges with Matthew Olzmann have expanded the scope of my writing (and when he suggested the collection needed one more poem, I wrote it and found the book's title). Rick Chess' generous responses to my work kept me attuned to the sacred parts of this practice. The wisdom of Nin Andrews, Susanne Paola Antonetta, Bruce Beasley, Esther Lin, Amy Peterson, and Frank Paino guided me through key moments of creation. Lauren Winner cast the deciding vote for *unalone*.

Friendship has held and helped me through these often-tumultuous years: Rick Chess; Jennifer Coon, EJ Wallman, and Mimi & Miles Coon (z"l); Jehanne Dubrow; Tessa Fontaine & Jeremy Morris; Jennifer Franklin; Luke Hankins; Cullen Covington-Hicks; Candice & Jerry Jacobs; Thomas & Mackenzie Kozak; K.T. Landon; Amy Peterson; Michael & Lizzie Shroff; Katie Storey & James Nestor; and Yerra Sugarman.

My Asheville writing group—Maggie Anderson, Nickole Brown, Gary Hawkins, Eric Nelson, and Rachel Shopper—gave helpful feedback and encouragement early on.

Long live editors who edit! Sophia Stid & Anna Lena Phillips Bell at *Ecotone*, Daniel Biegelson at *The Laurel Review*, Jessica Faust at *The Southern Review*, Matt Donovan for the anthology *The Map of Every Lilac Leaf: Poets Respond to the Smith College Museum of Art,* Ashley M. Jones for the anthology *What Things Cost: an anthology for the people*, Christina Shideler at *VIDA*, and Chloe Martinez at *Journal for Feminist Religious Studies*.

Rebecca Gayle Howell, Joy Ladin, Dorianne Laux, and Alicia Ostriker gave workshops that inspired a number of these poems.

Gratitude to the SunJune community of poets and to all my students—you continue to teach me long after our classes are through.

And thanks to the T.S. Eliot Foundation and the Dartmouth-Frost Place Poet-in-Residence program: the beauty and time at Eliot House and Frost Place made space for the final revision of these poems..

The experience of writing of this book led me to found Yetzirah: A Hearth for Jewish poetry, an organization that now thrives because of the generosity and great good work of Jehanne Dubrow, Rick Chess, Yerra Sugarman, Maya Bernstein, Jason Schneiderman, Shelby Sizemore, Cory Weller, and so many more who've set the foundation and continue to help us on our way, including Ilya Kaminsky, Alicia Ostriker, Rodger Kamenetz, Jacqueline Osherow, Victoria Redel, Jen Benka, and Eleanor Wilner. Gratitude to the growing community of Yetzirah poets, who buoys and inspires me daily.

Cassie Mannes Murray, thank you for x-raying this book down to its intentions and helping shepherd it into the world.

And Four Way Books: Sally Ball's suggestions and generative questions have made this a far better book than I could have created on my own. Martha Rhodes, your support and friendship mean more than you know. And big thanks to Ryan Murphy, Hannah Matheson, and, for her expert close-reading, Bridget Bell.

ABOUT THE AUTHOR

Jessica Jacobs is the author of *Take Me with You, Wherever You're Going* (Four Way Books, 2019), one of *Library Journal*'s Best Poetry Books of the Year, winner of the Devil's Kitchen and Goldie Awards, and a finalist for the Brockman-Campbell, American Fiction, and Julie Suk Book Awards; and *Pelvis with Distance* (White Pine Press, 2015), a biography-in-poems of Georgia O'Keeffe, winner of the New Mexico Book Award in Poetry and a finalist for the Lambda Literary Award; and is the co-author of *Write It! 100 Poetry Prompts to Inspire* (Spruce Books/Penguin RandomHouse, 2020). She is the founder and executive director of Yetzirah: A Hearth for Jewish Poetry.

PUBLICATION OF THIS BOOK WAS MADE POSSIBLE
BY GRANTS AND DONATIONS. WE ARE ALSO GRATEFUL
TO THOSE INDIVIDUALS WHO PARTICIPATED IN
OUR BUILD A BOOK PROGRAM. THEY ARE:

Anonymous (14), Robert Abrams, Michael Ansara, Kathy Aponick, Jean Ball, Sally Ball, Clayre Benzadon, Adrian Blevins, Laurel Blossom, Adam Bohannon, Betsy Bonner, Patricia Bottomley, Lee Briccetti, Joel Brouwer, Susan Buttenwieser, Anthony Cappo, Paul and Brandy Carlson, Dan Clarke, Mark Conway, Elinor Cramer, Kwame Dawes, Michael Anna de Armas, John Del Peschio, Brian Komei Dempster, Rosalynde Vas Dias, Patrick Donnelly, Lynn Emanuel, Blas Falconer, Jennifer Franklin, John Gallaher, Reginald Gibbons, Rebecca Kaiser Gibson, Dorothy Tapper Goldman, Julia Guez, Naomi Guttman and Jonathan Mead, Forrest Hamer, Luke Hankins, Yona Harvey, KT Herr, Karen Hildebrand, Carlie Hoffman, Glenna Horton, Thomas and Autumn Howard, Catherine Hoyser, Elizabeth Jackson, Linda Susan Jackson, Jessica Jacobs and Nickole Brown, Lee Jenkins, Elizabeth Kanell, Nancy Kassell, Maeve Kinkead, Victoria Korth, Brett Lauer and Gretchen Scott, Howard Levy, Owen Lewis and Susan Ennis, Margaree Little, Sara London and Dean Albarelli, Tariq Luthun, Myra Malkin, Louise Mathias, Victoria McCoy, Lupe Mendez, Michael and Nancy Murphy, Kimberly Nunes, Susan Okie and Walter Weiss, Cathy McArthur Palermo, Veronica Patterson, Jill Pearlman, Marcia and Chris Pelletiere, Sam Perkins, Susan Peters and Morgan Driscoll, Maya Pindyck, Megan Pinto, Kevin Prufer, Martha Rhodes and Jean Brunel, Paula Rhodes, Louise Riemer, Peter and Jill Schireson, Rob Schlegel, Yoana Setzer, Soraya Shalforoosh, Mary Slechta, Diane Souvaine, Barbara Spark, Catherine Stearns, Jacob Strautmann, Yerra Sugarman, Arthur Sze and Carol Moldaw, Marjorie and Lew Tesser, Dorothy Thomas, Rushi Vyas, Martha Webster and Robert Fuentes, Rachel Weintraub and Allston James, Abby Wender and Rohan Weerasinghe, and Monica Youn.